# THE RESCUE OF
# RIVER
# CITY

For Dave Lattker
Best Wishes to a
fellow American!

# THE RESCUE OF
# RIVER CITY

# DREW DIX

Drew Dix Publishing, Fairbanks, Alaska

For inquires contact Drew Dix Publishing web site:
www.drewdix.com

Library of Congress Card Number: 00-191508
ISBN 0-9703096-0-0

1. A Biography, Vietnam
2. Medal of Honor
3. Special Forces

Design: Image Studios, Colorado Springs, CO
Cover Photography: Drew Dix collection
Back Cover Photography: Drew Dix collection
Sculptor: David Dirrim
Sculpture Photography: John Suhay

Printed in the United States of America.

10 9 8 7 6 5 4 3 2 1    First Edition

For my parents
Faith and Harold Dix

and

"Professionals," Past, Present and Future

# CONTENTS

# FORWARD

I n Vietnam the first day of the New Year in the Chinese calendar is the biggest holiday of the year. It is called Tet, and in Vietnam Tet is as important to the Vietnamese as New Year's Day, Christmas, and the Fourth of July combined are to Americans. Tet is traditionally a holiday from work and even from warfare. Prior to 1968 the war stopped every year for three days to enable the soldiers from both sides to celebrate Tet with their families. In 1968, however, the Communists surprised the South Vietnamese and the Americans by taking advantage of the Tet holidays to surreptitiously infiltrate into the undefended cities and to occupy them. The initial success of this Viet Cong operation led many people, including some in the American media, to believe that the communists had won the war. Those people did not realize that the United States had soldiers like Special Forces Staff Sergeant Drew Dix, or that the South Vietnamese Government had the support of fighting units like the Provincial Reconnaissance Units, the PRU.

A few months before Tet of 1968 Drew Dix was assigned to be the PRU advisor in Chau Doc, a Provincial Capital with a population of almost 25,000 people situated in the Mekong Delta a few miles from the Cambodian border on the edge of a main tributary of the Mekong River. Cambodia served as a Viet Cong sanctuary and supply base, so Chau Doc was the most vulnerable city in South Vietnam to a surprise attack by the Viet Cong. The PRU were basically an armed intelligence collection unit with the mission of capturing Viet

Cong prisoners and documents, but they were so well trained and armed that many South Vietnamese province chiefs wanted to use them as assault units, so the PRU needed strong advisors to keep them from being misused. Drew had the respect of his province chief, so he had no such problems. Drew also had the strong support of Jim Monroe, an unflappable operations officer who was also a Special Forces Reserve Captain.

General George S. Patton once wrote, "In war nothing is impossible, provided you use audacity." At Tet in 1968 Drew had the audacity to attack a Viet Cong main force battalion that had infiltrated the city of Chau Doc while Drew and his PRU were on patrol near the Cambodian border. Within 56 hours Drew with the help of the PRU and some U.S. Navy Seals drove the Viet Cong battalion that they had decimated out of the city. He describes in fascinating detail how they did it in this book. The reader may wonder how Drew was able to recall all the details of his combat activities, but those who have been in combat know that the important details of intense combat activities are seared in the brain never to be forgotten.

In 1967-68 I was in charge of a number of activities in the Delta of Vietnam, including the operations of Jim Monroe and Drew Dix in Chau Doc. I mistakenly thought that Tet of 1968 would be a nice quiet time in the war for me to go on home leave, so I was back in the United States when the Viet Cong attacked the cities. I immediately terminated my home leave and received priority passage on a military aircraft to return to Vietnam. When I arrived at my headquarters in Can Tho, my deputy Andy Rogers briefed me on the situation throughout the Delta. Andy and I had both been parachute infantry officers in World War II and had seen combat as members of the OSS, The Office of Strategic Services, so we knew what it took for our military personnel to earn combat awards for their heroic activities at Tet. Andy saved his briefing on Drew Dix's activities until after he finished telling me about the bravery of the men we had who were wounded and those who deserved awards for outstanding heroism. When Andy had finished briefing me on Drew Dix's activities, I reacted as Andy expected and said, "Drew deserves nothing less then the Medal of Honor for what you just told me. Let's get General Timmes down here from Saigon to take the affidavits." Major General Charles Timmes was a retired general and a lawyer with prior experience in Vietnam as the deputy to General Harkins. General Timmes interviewed and took affidavits from eight people who had observed and were able to testify to Drew's courageous actions. About a year later President Johnson presented Drew Dix with the Medal of Honor.

I have long been aware of the highlights of what Drew Dix did at Chau Doc in Tet of 1968, but I was not previously aware of the details. This book is full of fascinating detailed descriptions of the multitude of combat actions in which Drew was engaged over that 56 hour period. It is a true tale of exciting and deadly combat, not a tactical textbook, but students of warfare can learn a great deal from it, particularly on the importance of shock action, rapid mobility, and the use of hand grenades and firepower in urban warfare. I think everyone interested in military combat will find this book fascinating. Anyone who likes to read an exciting tale will find it difficult to put the book down before finishing it.

I knew from personal experience that Drew could not have done what he did in Vietnam were he not in superb physical condition and totally combat ready as a result of the training he received in the Special Forces. In World War II in Burma as a member of Detachment 101 of the OSS I had commanded guerrilla forces composed of Kachin hill tribesmen behind Japanese lines and knew that I and most of my troops survived only because we were highly trained and in top notch physical condition. Many years later when I visited

Fort Bragg en route to Florida, I went for a run with Major Drew Dix and found him as fit as ever. He told me he generally ran about one to two hours a day to stay in shape. Drew had what it takes to be a good soldier: the training, the physical fitness, the courage, and the automatic response to meet whatever the challenge may be. On the walls of Special Forces units one frequently sees a sign that reads: "The difficult will be done immediately; the impossible may take a little longer." After reading Drew's book, that sign does not seem unrealistic. Achieving the impossible is a normal goal in warfare for people like Drew Dix.

James R. Ward
United States Department of State
(Retired)

# PROLOGUE

This is not a story about U.S. Army Special Forces. This is not a story about US Navy SEALs. This is not a story about the Central Intelligence Agency. This is not a story about Drew Dix. This is a story about a fifty-six hour period with "REAL WARRIORS" from those organizations during dangerous times in our history.

I ask myself why write about this now, 32 years after the Tet Offensive of Jan. 31-Feb. 1, 1968. The answer is clearly to explain my thought on how professional soldiers think, feel and perform in circumstances such as the one our country put us in. Vietnam was a major battle of the "Cold War." One of many where professional soldiers met the best the Soviets and the other Communist countries could throw at us. If we look at it that way, we can feel proud about our part in it. After all we won the war with the Soviet Union.

Communist ideology is one that practices total indoctrination and control of the people. Its unrelenting pressure on the population makes the battlefield a difficult place for conventional units to operate. Vietnam was no different. In fact this practice of total control of the people, either by indoctrination or through terror tactics, was extremely effective.

The United States Government, recognizing this, attempted to combat its effectiveness by establishing units such as the one I found myself assigned to. While in the pipeline as a Special Forces replacement, I was pulled out of the normal replacement channels and quickly sent to Saigon for enrollment in this program.

Immediately, I realized that I would soon be given the chance to put all of my Special Forces training and skills to good use. I would be tasked as a sole American to an armed intelligence-collection unit operating with three different ethnic elements. While the units were extremely effective with minimal exposure to U.S. conventional units, it was simply too little too late.

This story is told from my perspective only. I was fortunate to have been a member of the United States Army Special Forces throughout most of my 20-year military career. As a member of that organization, I had the honor to work closely with the special operations elements of the other services and with other agencies within our government.

The motto of the 5th Special Forces, "The Professionals" tells it all. Each of our country's elite forces are just that, "Professionals," and the way we are affected by war or our mission is different from how it affects the draftee or recruit. We do what it takes to get the job done and are affected little by political influences. At least we like to think we are not affected by politics. The seriousness with which we undertook our mission does not lessen the fact that the war in Vietnam was not managed right but it was simply managed too much.

Undertaking a task such as this book comes with a lot of responsibility. In order to reconstruct the events of 30 and more years ago, many calls and meetings were made to and with old friends. The best part of this undertaking was the renewal of these friendships. I thank each of them for their input.

Nevertheless, after 30 years, memories fade and some recollections do differ slightly. If I have offended anyone, it was not done intentionally. I wrote this the way I remembered it. In some accounts it was my opinion only of how the dialogue went.

Another significant point is that the omission of anyone does not mean they didn't perform. I simply didn't remember what took place or I was not present. For example, when the SEALs were not in town, I wasn't aware of what they were doing during this time. I am sure they must have been busy with the enemy where ever they were. I have come to the conclusion that if 10 people are shot at while attacking the same enemy position, the story becomes very personal and is viewed from each individual's own perspective.

When being processed out from Vietnam in Saigon, I had the good fortune to have been given copies of a few of the statements written for my Medal of Honor award. The statements that were given to me were written by Jim Moore (aka, Jim Monroe), Bynum Westall, Maggie Francot, Guy Nixon, Arturo Gatpayat, Prudencio Tolibas, Harry Humphries, Frank Thornton and others not mentioned in this book. These statements were prepared less than 30 days after the events and not 30 years. Even then, some of them differ slightly.

Whoever that Army specialist fifth class was who handed me the packet of statement in an envelope with General Timmes' name on it, I thank him. If it had not been for those statements, I may not have begun this undertaking.

Most of the participants in this account were young. This reminds us that it is the young who our country depends on. If this account does nothing else, it should be a reminder of the sacrifices made by our country's young. This in no way suggests that we should never get involved in war, but reminds us, that when we go to war, we must do it like we mean it.

We'll always have "Professionals" willing to go. After all the excitement and adventure is what makes this country so great, but let's save their enthusiasm for doing great things for those missions worth doing. We don't have an endless supply of young professionals.

One may ask while reading this book, how is it that someone so young is selected for an assignment like this. Training! When I went to Vietnam I was confident that I had the best training in the world and was trained by the best warriors in the world. Our country had been in Vietnam for eight years by then. Many of these trained warriors came back and passed on their skills to us. That is absolutely the only good thing about dragging a war on like we did there.

Unconventional warfare means that you organize, train and lead indigenous troops against enemy armed forces. To accomplish this, one must be trained in all types of weapons, equipment and tactics for waging war anywhere in the world or at least in the Theater of Operations where you will be sent.

Sure you usually have others serving with you. My assignment was unique in that I was selected to perform a mission as the only American in the field. For whatever reason I was selected, I thank those responsible for giving me the opportunity for that experience and having the confidence in me to let me have a crack at it.

I have had the great fortune to have participated in other challenging jobs. Like many others who have served in war, we have experienced the greatest challenges of our lives. Whether these experiences are good or not, is not the real question. The act of going to war is so significant in a young person's life that it is hard to top. For many, returning is a bad experience simply because the recognition for what they had experienced was not there. I, more than most, have been recognized many times and have had the opportunity, on each occasion, to say how proud I am to have served our country!

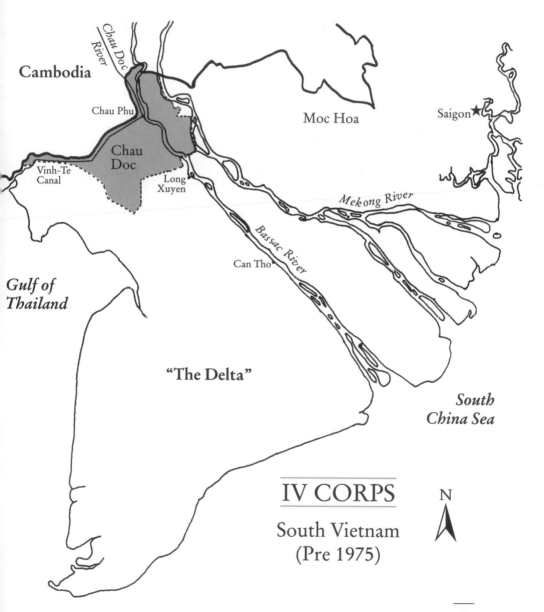

**Cambodia**

Chau Doc River

Chau Phu

Chau Doc

Vinh-Te Canal

Long Xuyen

Moc Hoa

Saigon ★

Mekong River

Bassac River

Can Tho

**Gulf of Thailand**

"The Delta"

**South China Sea**

# IV CORPS

South Vietnam
(Pre 1975)

N

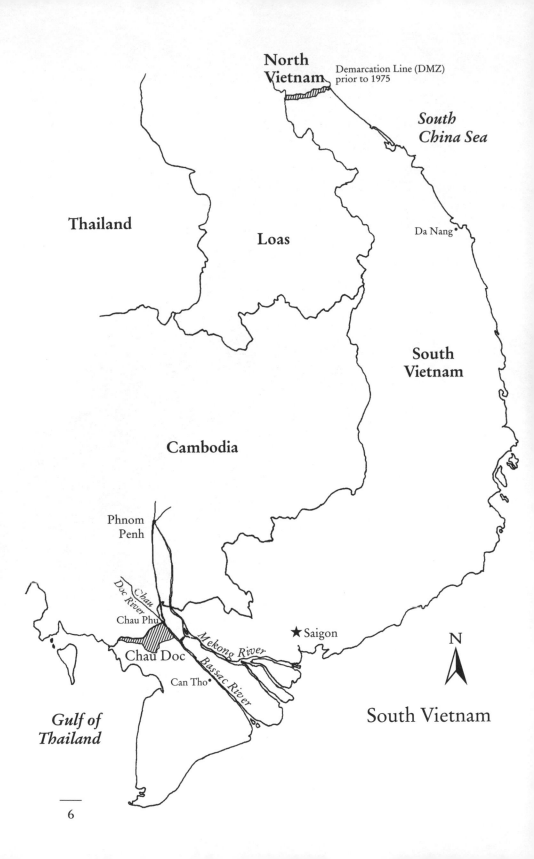

# CHAPTER 1

## WHERE HAVE THE VC GONE?

It had been an unusually dark night but now that the sun began to rise, the city of Chau Phu slowly emerged in the morning twilight. Looking in that direction, I could begin to make out the two- and three-story buildings of the downtown area as the sun softly reflected off of them.

We were just completing a five-day patrol along the Cambodian Frontier. They say a successful reconnaissance patrol is one you complete without being detected. Not in our case though. The mission of the Provincial Reconnaissance Unit (PRU) was to capture the enemy, and this time we were coming back empty-handed.

Approaching the steep mud bank of the Vinh Te Canal, I glanced back to see if the rest of my patrol was right behind me. Seeing they were, I sidestepped down the bank and eased myself into the warm, thick water. I could sense the six PRU were to my rear, uncovering the two sampans we had stashed late last evening. It was just a few short yards across the canal and we'd be back in Vietnam, and a few hundred meters more and we'd be at the edge of the city.

Without looking back, I took my place in the center of the first sampan just as Phat pushed us off. The Vinh Te was clearly on the Vietnam side of the border, but to us the canal represented the border since the actual line was hard to pick out. It was located somewhere further to the northwest about 200 to 300 hundred meters.

I wasn't sure if anyone actually could tell which country they were in, including the locals who freely traveled between the two countries. To them it didn't really matter. The border was just an arbitrary line that divided real estate that was connected by thousands of years of culture, religion and blood.

The PRUs skillfully maneuvered the small and incredibly unstable craft out into the canal as only the locals, whom the U.S. military called the "indigenous," could do.

Chau Phu city was the provincial capital for Chau Doc Province. The name of the city often was referred to by the provincial name of Chau Doc not only by Americans but the indigenous as well. The province, as well as the city, had a strong Cambodian influence. The names Chau Phu and Chau Doc were of Cambodian origin, from when this area was part of Cambodia, which added to the mystique of this part of the country.

Chau Phu, a city of about 25,000 people, was conveniently located less than a mile from the Cambodian border, allowing the Viet Cong easy access to this provincial capital.

Using the border as a sanctuary, they could run their secret government with little interference. In fact they virtually ran this province as well as Long Xuyen Province, which bordered Chau Doc to the south, through this secret infrastructure. The Viet Cong combined these two provinces into one communist province known as VC An Giang Province.

The proximity of the border made an excellent hunting ground for us. The primary mission of the Provincial Reconnaissance Unit was to put pressure on the enemy by eliminating the Viet Cong infrastructure, specifically its leadership. That is what we were out to do on this particular operation. I was hoping to snatch two officers who we knew frequently moved between Chau Doc Province and their headquarters in Cambodia.

When we didn't have success in locating our primary target, we almost always could pick up a low-ranking tax collector or one of the many recruiters who frequently traveled this area. I seldom came back empty-handed. It was easy enough to set up along the river or the Vinh Te canal and wait for one of these souls to pass by. Sometimes we simply would paddle our sampan down the canal or river with me covered up in the middle looking like a pile of cargo. The VC tax collector would signal with a single shot for us to come over where he would confiscate a part of the load as "tax." As we approached the bank, we would jump up and ruin his day. If he was alone and didn't resist, we disarmed him and brought him back. If there was a fight, we were ready.

This time we tried everything with no luck. There had been a suspicious absence of enemy activity of any kind during the past few days.

The two sampans gently nosed onto the opposite bank a few hundred meters from where we had requisitioned them the day before. Without saying a word, the seven of us moved up the bank and headed toward the edge of the city. We began to hear the morning sounds of Vietnam. Dogs were barking, roosters could be heard in the distance and chickens scurried for cover as we spooked them.

Out in the countryside when we approached the outskirts of any village at night, I always had the feeling the locals knew we were there. They seemed to know what was going on but never indicated they did. The fact that they waited to come out of their hooches until we passed was evidence enough for me. They knew by the night sounds, or the lack of them, that someone who didn't belong there was present. I'm sure it was the same for the Viet Cong.

We almost always operated at night and I felt comfortable knowing we could handle ourselves in the security of the darkness. The night was ours.

As we moved closer to the city and daylight started to intensify, I actually put myself on special alert. My troops were good but they didn't have the same respect for the daylight that I had. Maybe they also could tell by the morning sounds that all was well. I know that on this day I would have felt a lot better if we had seen some enemy activity.

The lack of enemy presence bothered me as we skirted the first Government of Vietnam (GVN) ambush site. It didn't take long to figure out that there weren't any friendlies to worry about this time either. Not seeing the normal sign of friendly activity added to my concern. Our Vietnamese allies routinely placed these ambushes in the exact same spot each night on the likely avenues of approach to the city. Because of that, they were easy to detect.

Nevertheless, I still had to be careful. I didn't want to run into one of these positions on our way back from an operation. I purposely avoided coordinating my movements with the Vietnamese units and since there usually weren't any U.S. units operating in the area, they didn't concern me.

Letting the Vietnamese know our plans was just too risky. To do so would certainly mean a security leak. We operated way beyond any support and usually in five- to eight-man patrols. Our most reliable security was absolute secrecy. Nobody was going to bail us out if we got into trouble.

In an attempt to find out what we were up to, the Vietnamese province chief—under the pretense of concern for our safety—often tried to pressure us to let him know where we were operating. He claimed that his patrols might accidental ambush one of our patrols.

I had my suspicions that the VC had penetrated the Vietnamese command, and we just couldn't take the chance. When enough proof was gathered, I was going to take care of that problem too.

Until then, the friendly ambushes didn't pose much of a threat to us. They were easy to navigate around or we simply waited until daylight to approach. This was done more as a courtesy to the province chief. It didn't look good for us to be able to move through their ambushes undetected. Even if we told them we'd wait until daylight, we could always move through their area at night if we needed to. This was about as political as we chose to be.

Keeping everyone guessing worked to our advantage. It also allowed us to establish enough rapport to keep them thinking everything was normal. Then when enough evidence was gathered against a VC infiltrator among the ranks, we could move in and take him.

To be able to operate in this fashion, I posed as a civilian. Much to the aggravation of both the Vietnamese and U.S. military, my civilian status was one of convenience. It allowed me to operate without the need to coordinate. The Vietnamese, and to a lesser degree the Americans, were extremely rank-conscious. There was absolutely no way a staff sergeant in the Army could get away with operating the way I needed to.

This morning was different. There were no signs of the usual ambushes so we pushed on through. It was beginning to look like both sides had decided to take time off for the Tet holidays. I was developing a gut feeling that this was going to be a hell of a Chinese New Year celebration.

Dropping to one knee, I signaled to Phat by raising one finger and motioned for him to move up to my position. Not knowing whether I had seen anything or not, he cautiously moved to where I was kneeling. I simply wanted to pause a minute to take a closer look at our route. We were about to enter a small village and had to pass between two rows of hooches that lined the dirt road leading into the main city.

These little communities, or hamlets, had their own local leadership. It was in these small population clusters that the VC had the most influence. The people of these hamlets were completely on their own, especially at night. Often they supported the VC with food, supplies, shelter and information—much as they did for me and my troops. It was clear both sides used the civilians to get to each other.

I looked over the approach and thought one of these days we are going to get hit moving back to our camp. For this reason, I made a special effort to treat the people closer to our home a little better. I did so in a manner that maintained the proper balance of respect and fear. There is a thin line between the two strategies. To show concern and respect for them was good for long-term results, while demanding power and respect was definitely needed for immediate self-preservation.

I looked for Phat to give me some assurance that he thought it was clear. We never had to say much while on patrols and developed an understanding for what the other was thinking. Seeing no sign from him, I just shrugged my shoulders which Phat understood, making a similar gesture.

I had to admit to myself that this lack of activity on both sides made me a bit uneasy. It didn't seem to bother Phat or the others but then again nothing seemed to bother them when we were near our base camp. I'd just put it in the back of my mind until I could talk it over with Jim and Westy at the Embassy House. We just needed to cross one more monkey bridge and we'd be back.

We reached the actual city limits and now were moving between one- and two-story concrete buildings that lined an old paved street. In its day, this city and its streets were among the finest in Vietnam and certainly among the most picturesque. The French influence left over from better days long past was evident.

I began to get a faint whiff of the fresh French bread that seemed to be a part of the daily ritual in every village across the country. Chau Phu was no different. I could hear the whine of the three-wheeled Lambros as they raced through the old uneven streets of downtown delivering their loads of fresh bread. These drivers, I was sure, reported our every move as we proceeded through the streets toward the Embassy House.

The Delta was one continuous information network. This plus the extremely valuable rice harvest provided the perfect ingredients for guerrilla warfare. It often was said that whoever controls the Delta, which is the breadbasket of the region, would control Southeast Asia.

The conflict in the southern part of the Delta was being fought more as a guerrilla war than the conventional war being fought further north. Only on rare occasions did the VC main force choose to assemble and fight in large units as they were doing in the north. This didn't mean the war in the Delta was less deadly. In fact, the tactics used by the VC were extremely effective without provoking a really big buildup of conventional forces. Whenever they chose to test their strength, they suffered severe losses.

Our interval subconsciously closed up as we left the dusty dirt road that led us through the poorer area and into the main part of the city. Other than the river, there were only two main approaches to the city: the one from the south where the Embassy House was located and the one from the west.

The short dirt road we used to get into the city from the northwest was of lesser importance. It couldn't be used for anything other than foot travel or two- or three-wheeled vehicles and they could only go as far as the canal we had just crossed.

All of the roads leading to the city were lined with one- or two-room, wood-framed, rough-looking buildings exactly like the ones we had just passed. They had thatched or tin roofs and were constructed of whatever materials that were handy at the time. They were a far cry from the buildings that made up the main part of the city, which we were now entering.

We made our way through the downtown center as the road widened and turned into a heavily shaded street that followed the Bassac River. A long, narrow park with numerous shade trees ran between the street and the river. The overall setting seemed out of place considering that a very brutal war was being waged throughout the countryside. Whenever I passed through this part of the city, I often lost sight of that fact for a few moments.

We had only about 1,200 meters- about three quarters of a mile to go before we reached the Embassy House. First we had to pass by the Vietnamese military headquarters and the hospital.

The street narrowed somewhat as we left the park. Now, passed the hospital, we turned onto a dusty road lined with small houses and a few shops. The only large structures from there until we reached the Embassy House was the large house, adjacent to the Embassy House, occupied by the American Senior Provincial Advisor, and the impressive white structure that was the Catholic Church directly across the street.

As the Embassy House came into view, one of the PRUs ahead of me, wanting a quick breakfast, snatched a couple of loaves of warm bread from the bunch that hung like bananas from the shop porch. Upon reaching the owner, I handed the old man a 100-piaster note to cover his loss. He immediately handed me two more loaves and bowed slightly as he hopped along subserviently for a couple of meters, thanking me.

The idea that power in this country means so much was hard for me to get used to. My troops seemed to take advantage of this whenever they could. Hell, it's their country, I thought. Who am I to try to change a thousand years of history? The problem I had was of more concern. Where the hell had all the VC gone?

Approaching the Embassy House, I couldn't help but notice the change that had taken place since I had left five days earlier. It was becoming more like a compound or fortress instead of the rather plain upper-class French house we were living in.

Bynum P. Westall, or Westy as we called him, has been working on the house with the tenacity of a beaver since I had arrived in-country three and a half months earlier. But the progress in the past five days, since I left with Phat and his men, was remarkable. Westy's eagerness to handle the construction aspect of our program was welcomed by Jim Moore and myself. It left more time for us to deal with the pressing operational situations.

Westy often took heat from us for his constant talk of the next project. We had the attitude to just let him do it. Nevertheless, Westy had systematically attacked the project and transformed this place into a defendable position. The compound was now enclosed with an eight-foot wall. In the front, the wall was actually two walls built two feet apart and filled with sand, providing sufficient strength to withstand a direct hit from a rocket attack.

Along this wall, shooting ports were cut about every five feet. On the north corner was a bunker shaped in a half-circle that extended out into the street much like the turret of an English castle. A guard could position himself on top or in the bottom section and have a good view of what was coming or going on the street that ran in front of the compound. When needed, he could take up a position below and fire out the shooting ports that were there as well.

I often felt the actual location of the Embassy House was not selected by chance. Everything in our business was carefully thought out.

Across the street was the church that supported the rather large number of Catholics in the Delta. The VC did not want to risk alienating this segment of the population at this time by destroying the church (which would certainly happen if they chose to make a serious effort to take us out). Of course if the situation changed, as it often did in the Delta with regard to religious factions, then that theory soon would be outdated and the church would become a fortress for them to hit us from.

The river was to our east and at this point was about a mile wide. Across the river was a small Government of Vietnam (GVN) outpost built in the center of a hamlet like the one we had just passed through.

The road that ran in front of the Embassy House paralleled the river in both directions. Where the compound was located, the river and the road almost touched. Only the compound itself separated them.

Toward the south the road headed off at a slight angle so from the roof we could fire our crew-served weapons—machine guns and mortars—down the road for almost 600 to 700 meters and cut off any enemy force attempting to maneuver on us from that direction. The heavy weapons procured a few weeks earlier found a good home here and topped off the defensive plan for our compound.

I wondered if Westy knew something we didn't because of the seriousness with which he took on the construction project or whether he just felt the need for the extra security. After all he did run the Provincial Interrogation Center (PIC) and the Police Special Branch. I guess he could very well know something. I had been providing him plenty of customers for the PIC in the past weeks. This time was different. Westy wasn't going to get anyone new to interrogate. It would have been nice to have had some fresh information to explain the lack of enemy activity.

As I approached the gate, Vinh, one of the 16 Chinese Nungs we had to help defend the Embassy House, climbed off his perch and opened the recently installed large steel gate, freshly painted a light green. Vinh, always with a grin on his face, was the senior Nung guard selected to that position either because he was the oldest or because he was the best marksman of the group. He seemed especially proud of the new addition.

Phat and the other Cambodians in the patrol continued on down the road toward the PRU compound, located adjacent to the proposed airport on the outskirts of town.

Not saying a word, each passed me making his own obscene gesture as to what he was going to do with (or maybe to) the wife or girlfriend. Again, we were able to communicate even the most personal messages without the need to say very much. We could spend days together on an ambush or a prisoner snatch and not say more than a few words the entire time. I smiled and made my own gesture, which got a laugh out of all of them.

After I entered, Vinh, all four and a half feet of him, leaned against the heavy door and pushed it closed. He saluted and smiled as he quickly scrambled back to his post on top of the corner bunker.

"Where're Mr. Westall and Mr. Moore?" I called back to Vinh.

Saying nothing, he pointed toward the rear of the compound. Westy was walking toward me from the radio room located near the rear of our compound, or I should say fortress. Westy, a man in his 40s, dressed in a light sport shirt and khaki pants, looked more like a businessman on vacation than a lieutenant colonel in the Army. He was always in a hurry looking for one of the Nungs or one of the many Vietnamese workers he had on the payroll for camp construction.

"Where's Jim?" I asked.

"How'd the operation go, Drew?" Westy yelled over some major construction noise.

"It went OK, Westy, but I need to run a few things by you and Jim. Where is he anyway?"

"Back in the radio room talking on the single side-band with Saigon. Let's go find him," Westy said as he headed to the rear office.

I told him, "I'll be right with you after I drop off some of this gear I've been carrying around for the last five days."

I tossed my web gear into my room. Just then Nago, approached and said, "Gimmie Swedish-K. We clean for you," acting somewhat annoyed that it apparently hadn't been fired on this trip.

"OK, Nago," I told him. "How have you guys been?"

"OK, Mr. Drew," he said. "Next time Nago can go with you?"

"Yeah, Nago," I replied. "Maybe two or three days we go."

Smiling, he took off with my Swedish-K slung over his shoulder. The Chinese Nungs were damn good troops I thought as I watched him scurry off toward their living quarters.

I wished I could take the Nungs on all of my operations but I needed local Vietnamese or Cambodians to get me through the villages undetected. That was the only way we could be effective in surprising our infrastructure targets that often blended into the hamlets and villages. The Nungs spoke very little Vietnamese and what they did probably would give us away. The ones who spoke Vietnamese did so with a heavy North Vietnamese accent. Most of the Nungs we had were born in the northern provinces of North Vietnam or on Hinan, an island province of China.

Jim and Westy were already huddled around a map as I approached. Jim Moore was wearing a customized uniform that looked somewhat like U.S. Army jungle fatigues dyed black. No doubt they were made for him by one of the local tailors. This uniform was designed to be practical, right down to the pocket on his upper right sleeve that held a basic load of cigars, one of which he had in his mouth as he spoke.

Jim looked up and with a heavy Southern accent said, "Hey, Drew, how'd it go over there?" It was obvious why many of his associates called him "Alabama".

"Well, Jim, I don't really know," I told him. "There wasn't much going on. In fact we didn't even see the usual friendly activity. It was like everyone in this country knows something is going on, except us."

"Do the PRUs know anything?" Jim asked.

"I don't think so," I replied. "They know that many people have moved into the city for Tet. If they have, they're already here because, as I said, there wasn't much movement out there in the last day or so. I'm going to the house and wash some of this Vinh Te mud off my butt."

"OK, Drew," Jim said.

"I'll have Co Tu make some breakfast for you," Westy volunteered.

Not saying a word, I moved off.

The Embassy House was structured around the three of us. Westy, an Army lieutenant colonel on loan to the CIA, managed the day-to-day administration of the House along with being the advisor to the Police Special Branch and the Provincial Interrogation Center (PIC). Westy ran the police side of the House so accordingly, he was the "P" Officer.

The PIC was the organization that received captured enemy soldiers or members of the infrastructure for initial interrogation. If the prisoner turned out to be important, he would be transferred up the system to undergo a more sophisticated interrogation. The idea was that we could get information we could use before the prisoners were moved up the ladder. Once they left, we rarely got any timely feedback. The next step up from province level was to the corps. In our case it was IV Corps.

The Corps headquarters was located in Can Tho, about an hour's helicopter ride to the south or, if needed, we could take our Boston Whalers and make it in three hours.

Our Regional Headquarters also was in Can Tho. Mr. James R. Ward was the Regional Officer in Charge (ROIC). He was a dynamic individual with a colorful background that began with Detachment 101 of the Office of Strategic Services (OSS) in Burma during World War II and now was an officer with the U.S. "State Department."

Remembering when I first arrived in Vietnam, I was briefed before going to Chau Doc by several supporting elements of the program and given a welcoming interview with Mr. Ward. His advice made a lasting impression on me. He began by telling me about his experiences in Burma, fighting the Japanese, in a unit that had some similarities to the one I was going to. The most valuable advice was concerning how to work with the local population.

He said that it is important to take charge early on but always look and listen to them: "They often know more than they let on. They can keep you alive or they can get you killed! Never let your guard down."

Since operating as a lone American in a mercenary unit of almost 150 was new to me, this information was having a special impact. Since I had a fairly large unit at my disposal, he made a special point to emphasize the importance of decentralizing the intelligence collection efforts.

Upon asking him what would be the standards by which I would be judged, he simply responded, "Drew, you know what needs to be done, so go out and do it. The only time you'll hear from us is if you aren't producing results. If you need anything, call us but you have a good man in the province with you," referring to Jim Moore.

I left his office thinking that I'd died and gone to heaven. What more could a guy ask for? A trained field soldier with "mission orders". I had better enjoy this since it was doubtful I'd ever have this much freedom to operate on my own again.

Jim Moore, as he was known then, was a career CIA employee. I knew at the time he was using an alias, but it was many years later, not until after he had retired, that others knew his true identity to be Jim Monroe.

Jim was the advisor to CG and the RD programs. The Census Grievance (CG) program was intended to be a connection between the local civilian population and the government and a vehicle to air grievances. This cadre of individuals was integrated within the population down to the smallest hamlet. The general idea was that they would keep us informed on the problems that concerned the people.

It was a part of the "win the hearts and minds program" but I doubted its success as far as its intended mission. It was, however, valuable in providing information that could be used for intelligence purposes. Often the information we received from them led us to VC infrastructure or to confirm information that had been collected.

Jim also was the advisor to the RD Cadre (Revolutionary Development). These guys were an armed group who worked in the hamlets and villages where they lived. They did civil projects such as constructing wells and sanitation systems or whatever was the social priority at the time. It was a common belief by those of us in the field that these units were marginally successful. I believed they also were far more useful in providing information or to confirm information we had received from other sources for intelligence purposes.

While Westy had the appearance of being the senior person at the Embassy House, Jim clearly ran things as well as supervising the operational side of the outfit and therefore was known as the "O" officer.

While I was hired to run the PRU, I reported to Jim. The Provincial Reconnaissance Unit (PRU) was an armed intelligence-collection unit with the primary mission to capture VC infrastructure, that is to say VC leaders. What that allowed me to do was react on my own initiative without the need to coordinate with other units. Such "coordination" often guaranteed failure because of security leaks or by simply over-managing. The Vietnamese were famous for being extremely thorough. So thorough in fact that they seemed to plan until everyone knew what was going on and I mean everyone. The less others knew about what we were doing, the less likely we would be compromised.

As the PRU leader, I wore civilian clothes which reinforced my civilian status. The recruits for the PRU came from where ever I could find them. Many were former VC who turned themselves in or whom we had captured and convinced of the error of their ways.

The PRUs also had civilian status and were draft exempt, which meant that the Vietnamese government couldn't get their hands on them. This exempt status was especially useful when we were tracking down Viet Cong who got a little "too close to home." The Viet Cong had infiltrated every level of government and the military was no exception. It was my mission to become the biggest pain in the ass I could to the VC secret government.

As I walked back toward the main house, I couldn't keep from thinking about what a neat set-up we had here. It was a far cry from the average A-camp to which most Special Forces types like me were assigned and where I wanted to go when I first arrived in-country. I still wasn't sure how I was selected for this assignment. I remembered how I felt when I was pulled out of my group at Cam Rahn Bay when I first arrived in Vietnam and was told I would be going to Saigon. I thought at the time I was going to end up in some administrative job, passing out supplies or something. Only when I was given money to buy civilian clothes did I suspect there might be a bit more to this assignment. This isn't all bad, I thought, and my guilt about the accommodations must have been pretty shallow. An Army lieutenant colonel ordering breakfast for a staff sergeant seemed a bit weird, even though we were in civilian clothes. I could get used to it.

Jim, on the other hand, was a civilian but every now and then would put on a uniform of a Special Forces captain and go off for a couple days or a week, doing who knows what.

This was a hell of a way to fight a war but I knew we were effective. It allowed the greatest amount of U.S. influence with the least amount of risk to American soldiers. I was the only American leading 137 indigenous troops.

I liked the concept of giving the locals the opportunity to fight for their country. By this time my unit was averaging more than 40 captures a month. This had to have been hurting the VC infrastructure.

As the days of sweat and stench from wading in the Vinh Te Canal started flowing down the drain, Jim knocked on the door: "Drew, I just got a radio message from Can Tho."

"What do they want?" I asked as I pulled back the curtain.

"They asked if we'd like to have a SEAL platoon to work with. What do you think, Drew? It's your call. It seems that this platoon is looking for some action and they're not getting much down south."

"Hell yes, Jim," I told him. "I'd like to have some company on some of my ops. It would be good to have some round eyes to talk with. The SEALs have some shit-hot equipment. I bet they could even have some brown-water Navy support, too (referring to the river forces as opposed to the regular surface or blue-water Navy). If they are as good as the guys we worked with a while back, we damn sure can use them. When are they due in?"

"They were coming up anyway and have already left Binh Thuy," Jim replied. "They could be here anytime. It's still your call on whether you want them or not."

"I understand," I said. "Let's see how it goes, but from what I know, it damn sure can't hurt. We both know that something's in the wind and the extra firepower might come in handy."

Just then we could hear the deep-throated sound of the Navy boats positioning themselves around the small docks just out from the radio room behind the house on the Bassac River.

I grabbed a towel and draped it around my neck and pulled on a clean pair of tiger-stripe camouflaged pants and headed toward the docks. As Jim and I approached, I could see two PBRs (patrol boat river) tied up and two waiting their turn out in the middle of the river. I hadn't realized that the docks Westy had engineered would be needed this soon.

Just then several tiger-suited guys began throwing gear down onto the docks. One of the PBR skippers yelled, "Is it all right to tie up here?"

"Sure," yelled Westy, as he hurried down to greet our guests. Westy no doubt was in his glory, seeing how useful his docks were.

I had to admit the PBRs were a formidable war machine. With a crew of five, they were about 32 feet long, powered by twin diesels. Each was armed with twin .50-caliber machine guns on the bow and one at the stern, and some were equipped with mortars.

It looked like one had a Honeywell on the pedestal just aft of the cabin in place of an M-60 machine-gun. The Honeywell is a hand-cranked 40-millimeter grenade launcher that fired somewhat like an army Gattling gun used during the Indian wars.

As the two boats maneuvered in large circles out in the river, I thought how much they resembled PT boats of World War II. Constructed on the same principle, they were built for speed and fire-power rather than with heavy armament. Instead of the plywood of their predecessors, they were constructed of fiberglass. I sure liked the concept and it was going to be good having them around.

# CHAPTER 2

## A LITTLE COMPANY TO BRING IN THE NEW YEAR

The first SEALS were making their way up the stairs to the guard position overlooking the river. When one of them walked up I could see it was Dick Marcinko. If he had the same platoon we worked with a few weeks back, they would be a big help in the coming days. They were a good bunch of guys and would do about anything.

Marcinko was all right, but had a unique leadership style and seemed to be a bit too interested in his future, in my opinion. A person gets the feeling that most of what he says and does is an act and done for impact, especially his crudeness. I don't want anyone to think the rest of us were a bunch of choirboys, but we had dubbed him "THE MOUTH," which I think he liked. The fact that he ran his platoon the way he did and it still functioned so well attested to the character of the individuals in the unit.

I recognized several members of the platoon as they made their way up the steps. Yeah, it was the same platoon: "Good to have you back in River City, Hoss. Hey, Jack, ready to go after some bad guys?"

Hoss Kucinski, the senior enlisted man in the platoon, just smiled as he started giving assignments. He was always right down to business and never wasted words.

Jack Saunders was steady and I liked having him around. He always seemed to add a bit of common sense to any issue. Jack walked up while reaching out his hand and said, "Good to be back, Drew."

Then there was Rex Johnson, who had a fascination with weapons. In fact he liked them so much he hounded me to trade him a Walther PPK I had but didn't use for a Ruger .357 Buntline.

There was Doc Nixon, Ted Risher and Harry "The Hump" Humphries. Harry was a level-headed operator whom the platoon respected. He was a stud and gave the impression he could handle himself in about any situation and worked real well under pressure. Additionally, he had one great sense of humor.

Doc was a Navy corpsman assigned to the platoon. It would be good having a real medic around. I did OK treating my troops. The cross-training I received from our A-Team medic back at Fort Bragg already had proven useful; but I had to admit it would be nice having someone around who could patch me up if I needed it.

The assistant platoon commander, an ensign and the only other commissioned officer, was Gordy Boyce. I liked him and thought he would be a good hand in a fire-fight. He was the type person you knew would always come through when the chips were down. I felt that the rest of the platoon liked him and respected him, which was saying a lot because young officers throughout the services in Vietnam were viewed with skepticism—at least until they proved themselves in-country.

As the others started up the steps, I was glad the entire platoon was back, including Silver, a white 90-pound German Shepherd, with his handler, (Schwalenberg). There was Frank Scollice and Dennis Drady too.

Jim directed some of the men to his quarters, saying, "I've got plenty of room upstairs where you guys stayed before."

"Hoss," I said, "there's room on the roof if you want to put some of the guys up there. We've got a new toy up there (referring to the .50-caliber machine gun we recently added to our arsenal). You might want to assign someone to it. There's plenty of crew-served weapons to go around."

"OK," Hoss mumbled.

"How is it going. Dick?" I asked as Marcinko approached.

"OK, Drew, but the troops here need some action. The intel down south sucks and we keep coming up dry."

"I think we can fix you up," I told him. "You've come to the right place. You can go there (as I pointed east) for a little action. You can go there for a bit more (pointing in the opposite direction) or you can get more than you want if you just head there a couple of clicks."

"We'll stick with you for a while if that's OK. What about the Tet cease-fire that starts tonight?" Marcinko asked.

"I've got some ideas about that," I replied. "Let's talk about it after you guys get your gear put away and I get some chow. I've just come back from five days in the bush. See you in about three zero in the house."

"OK, Drew, that should give us enough time. I'll bring Hoss and Gordy."

Westy, Jim and I were about finished with breakfast when Dick, Hoss and Gordy walked in.

"You guys want something to eat?" Westy asked. "Co Tu can fix you up something."

Co Tu shuffled into the dining room upon hearing her name, somewhat embarrassed at seeing Marcinko dressed only in his navy swim shorts and sporting a lot of body hair. The Vietnamese don't have much and the sight of this big hairy American probably shocked the hell out of her.

"No, we're OK," Marcinko said as Co Tu blushed and scurried off to the kitchen.

"What you got going?" he asked, directing his question to Westy. Westy motioned to Jim, who responded.

"Drew here just came back from five days along the 'Red Line' and we were trying to figure out why there doesn't seem to be much activity. Drew thinks that something is going on. I guess I believe it too."

"That doesn't fit what we've been told by higher," said Marcinko.

Jim and Westy responded that they knew what headquarters was saying.

"They think this God-damned place is all but pacified," I added. "The number of bad guys the PRUs and I have been picking up these past weeks indicate that things are alive and well. We've averaged about 40 captures a month."

"That's right," Westy chimed in.

"What intelligence have your guys at the PIC been getting?" Jim asked.

Westy told him, "Well. Jim, there is an indication that there is something brewing. What that something is, I don't know. It seems that we down here in the trenches have an idea that something's going to happen and the folks in Saigon say the war is won in the Delta."

"What do our people say? I asked Jim, referring to the State Department and CIA channels.

"I think they are in agreement with us that we still have a war to fight here," Jim responded. "But I doubt if we are going to do much during these next few days because of this cease-fire."

"Does that mean I've got to stay holed up here and sit on my ass for the next couple of days?" I asked.

"No. Drew," Jim told me. "Do you have a plan?"

"Like I've been saying, there has been a lot of traffic along the border over the past few days and then it just dropped off, cold turkey! Westy here thinks the increase in traffic for a few days were relatives and friends moving in for the holidays. I talked with Bao just before breakfast and he feels a bit uneasy but doesn't have an answer. When Bao feels uneasy, I've learned to feel uneasy too.

"Dick," I said, "Bao is my PRU leader. He is 'number one.' This guy has been around for years and is a legend. The fact that he doesn't really want to take many troops on a recon mission right now tells me he knows something is up and doesn't want to weaken his position at the camp. He'll go if I want him to but maybe I don't have to take but a couple guys as guides."

"What do you mean?" Jim asked.

"Well Dick and his men are here for a little action and I can't think of a better way to accommodate them, if they're willing."

"God damn right we're willing," Dick responded. "My men are always ready!"

I knew they would be.

"When do you want to go?" he asked.

"Tonight at dark," I responded.

"We'll be ready."

"OK, Dick, you're on." I told him. "I'll just take a couple of my Cambodes to help us communicate and guide us in. I've got two in mind who are from that area and I've used them there before. Also, I'd like to use the PBRs if they're game."

"They'll go," Dick responded.

"They probably plan to patrol every night anyway and what

better way to do it than to support us. I like it." I told him.

Westy asked, "Drew, what about the cease-fire?"

Jim responded before I could: "Drew understands the program and isn't going to do anything that doesn't need to be done."

"Right, Jim," Westy quickly agreed. "Let's hear Drew's plan."

"OK," I said, and started outlining my ideas. "I plan to go up the Bassac several clicks where the Bassac comes into Vietnam using the PBRs. There's a stretch of uninhabited beach where we should be able to beach without being spotted. We need to use all four boats. We'll all board one.

"I want the boats to patrol in single file some distance apart like they were on a routine patrol. We'll make one pass and turn west at the border, like they normally would do. After we turn back toward Vietnam, we'll be a little closer to the shoreline. One boat, the one with us on it, will peel off and head into shore where we get off. After it drops us off, that PBR will return to the end of the column. If all goes well, we should be able to do this without being detected.

"From there, I plan to head toward the border about four clicks from where we're inserted. That will bring us near a small Cambodian outpost. I figure if something big is about to come down, there should be some activity near this outpost. The Cambodian unit there is very sympathetic to the local VC."

Marcinko replied, "Yeah, that should work. We've inserted that way before."

"Sounds like a plan, Drew," Jim responded. "Take care of yourself and good luck." He then asked, "When does the cease-fire go into effect?"

Westy responded, "Today. It went into effect this morning and it doesn't prohibit reconnaissance patrols anyway."

I added, "We'll do what we need to. Maybe we might come up dry, but somehow I don't think so. Dick, why don't you alert the skipper and I'll see you about 1730."

Marcinko and the two SEALs left the room.

Westy was expressing concern about the SEALs operating near the border. He said that it was one thing for Drew and the indigenous to poke around there, but for a U.S. unit to do so might cause a problem. As I left the two sitting at the table, I could hear Jim say, "Christ, Westy, don't worry about this op. It'll work out."

I'm glad politics weren't my problem. Operating was the only thing on my mind and I was thankful that was all there was for me to worry about, other than getting some badly needed sleep right now. A couple hours of rack time would be great. There hadn't been much time for rest over the past five days and we'd be up north for the next 24 hours at least.

Lying down on my bed, I couldn't help thinking about the upcoming operation. In the past three months I'd become comfortable operating by myself with only me and my PRUs to worry about. I really liked the concept of smaller units. After all, smaller units made smaller targets.

I've also become used to me being the only one I had to worry about. The PRUs always seemed to take care of themselves. Maybe they were nervous as hell and I just couldn't understand them. In any case, as it turned out, we took care of each other with little support. Now we'd be operating in no-man's land and there would be 12 of us not counting the PBRs. Large units were OK but along with large units came the usual fire support like air and artillery.

I wondered if Marcinko realized we wouldn't have air or artillery on this op. The SEALs usually operate with air support. They almost always have Seawolves (helicopter gunships) on call when they went out. If this insertion went undetected we'd probably get to the border without a problem. I was confident that we would be able to handle ourselves in the field. The only vulnerable part of this operation was the insertion. If the big wheels in Saigon were right, nothing was going to happen anyway. Yeah, right! I thought, as I dozed off.

I felt like I had been asleep for only a few minutes when I heard Jim at my door. He had just returned from meeting our scheduled courier flight from Can Tho.

"Drew, we've got more company," he said.

"Who is it?" I asked, wondering to myself what could be going on now.

"It's Frank Thornton. He was on the courier flight."

"Hey, Frank, are you here for the party?"

"Yeah, Drew. I went by Binh Thuy and heard that Marcinko was coming up here too."

Frank was a SEAL and also one of those guys you could count on when a fight was brewing. He wasn't assigned to Marcinko's platoon—or any other platoon for that matter. He was assigned to the Vietnamese SEALs as their advisor. I had worked with Frank before and knew him to be a real operator. Whenever the LDNNs (Vietnamese SEALs) weren't operating or were between training cycles, he would leave to find some action on his own. This time he came to us.

Jim said, "Frank said the LDNN's were off for the holidays," confirming what I thought.

Frank interrupted saying, "I didn't realize that Marcinko's platoon would be coming here also until just before I left."

No doubt he was on his own looking for some action but still didn't want to wear out his welcome.

"No problem, Frank," I told him. "There's always room for you."

I thought to myself that Frank never hesitated jumping into the action. He was an averaged-sized person with a scrappy kind of build and a decided New England accent. He was a really good hand in the field and I knew it would be helpful to have him around.

"Frank," I said, "you're just in time. We're leaving at dusk on the PBRs. I'm only taking two PRUs. You've worked with them before when we were operating along the border a while back. It's still a PRU operation though."

"Great," he replied. "I'll be ready to go when you are."

Hoss stuck his head in the doorway as we were finishing and asked if there were any changes in the plans. "The PBRs will be ready to go on time," he said. "They've got some maintenance to do first. We'll have one less on the PBR."

"Why's that?" I asked.

"Scollice has a real hoarse cough and can't control it. Doc has tried everything but nothing seems to work. We don't want to have him waking up the neighborhood," Hoss replied.

Good idea, I thought. We would have a hard enough time to keep from being seen traveling in such a large group. We damn sure didn't need to have our position compromised by someone who couldn't control a cough.

Several times, while with my PRUs, we've had to pack up and move because someone coughed or sneezed. When it happens, everyone simply gets up and moves. There is never any criticism of the individual. You just can't take the chance.

"Will they be ready to go at 1800 hours?" I asked.

"Yup," Hoss grunted, "that's a good time. Any special gear?"

"No," I told him. "I think just your normal gear. You could bring a couple silenced weapons if you have them with you."

"Right, we usually have at least one with us anyway."

"Great, I'll see you at 1800 hours then. Frank is going along so we'll still have the same number on the boat."

Not saying anything, Hoss ambled off.

It was now 1500 hours. I laid down again to try to get a couple more hours of rack time. I was anxious to get back out on the river to see what was going on and I really didn't want to be in town tonight. I wasn't in the holiday spirit and celebrating Tet just didn't seem like the thing to do with this war going on. Anyway I felt more comfortable in the field.

I woke up in what seemed like only a couple of minutes to the sound of the PBRs warming up. I looked at my watch; it was 1715 hours. I just needed a few minutes to get ready. I shuffled through some maps and selected those that would cover our area of operation. I grabbed my gear and as I opened the door, Nago handed me my Swedish-K and a fresh pouch of magazines.

"Here, Mr. Drew," he said. "When you come back, Nago can go?"

Remembering my earlier promise that he could go out with me soon, I told him, "Right, Nago, you can go. You a good man."

I gave him a thumbs up and we exchanged din hows as he responded with a similar thumbs up.

I headed down to the docks and the SEALs were already on board the second boat. I tossed my gear into the already crowded craft. If it wasn't for the necessity to go on one boat for the insertion, our all being together seemed a bit risky. I'm sure the others felt the same but didn't say anything.

The departure was uneventful and right on time. The water was extremely flat and there was a low cloud cover that would help block out the stars and moonlight later. This low light also would help us move up the river undetected.

The boats positioned themselves in a column the way we had discussed as they moved to the center of the river. The river from here on up to the border was about a mile to a mile and a half wide. This gave us fairly good protection from rocket or recoilless rifle attack. PBRs were vulnerable to these types of ambushes and several had been lost this way over the course of the war.

I was glad the skipper seemed cautious. The manner in which they moved out with minimum noise and radio traffic gave the impression that these were pro's. As we continued to move steadily up the Bassac, all on board settled in for the two- to three-hour trip to the border.

The night was extremely calm. There was not even the slightest breeze and the only sounds were the steady drone of the heavy engines and distant artillery firing flares from An Phu, the Vietnamese district headquarters to the north of us. No artillery explosions could be heard because of the cease-fire, which seemed kind of odd to me.

Occasionally the column would shut down and drift to look and listen for any enemy activity. This was their usual tactic and I was glad that on this night they didn't deviate from their normal procedures. We needed all the advantage of surprise we could manage. If the enemy was going to observe the cease-fire then they wouldn't regard our reconnaissance patrol as a threat.

It was getting close to 2130 hours as the skipper said the border was just ahead. It had taken us a little longer than I had originally planned but that wouldn't pose a problem at all. We would still be able to get in and out of the objective with plenty of time to spare before daylight.

"We'll be turning around soon and then we'll be at the insertion point in another 15 or 20 minutes."

"OK, skipper," I said and Marcinko responded with a "roger."

"You guys ready," I whispered.

"Ready" came a few muffled tones as the PBR moved in a wide arc at what must be the border.

Like near the Vinh Te where I was just a few hours ago, the "Proverbial Red Line", was nowhere to be seen to let the outsiders, like us, know where it was.

I was right; the cloud cover was perfect tonight. It was really getting dark. So far so good, I thought as our PBR slowly turned to the west and the distant bank began to come into focus.

The PBR slid onto the bank as our skipper skillfully stuck the heavy bow in the mud, securing it so we could climb off a stable platform. The mud along this stretch of the river was unlike any I've ever seen. It could grab hold of you so tight that it would take the rest of the platoon and a tractor to pull you out. The skipper no doubt knew that as we unloaded and lightened his load, he easily would come out of the mud.

I mentally checked my gear and gave the magazine in my Swedish-K a light slap at the bottom to make sure it was secure. We piled off without a word. The PBR backed off with little power under its now light load. This entire sequence took less than 30 seconds.

We spread out in a hasty defensive position waiting for the boat to get out of sight and for any sign that we had been detected. We hadn't and in another minute our small force moved out with one PRU as point and me a few steps behind. Silver and his handler were just behind me.

We entered a narrow band of bamboo that bordered the river. As we emerged from the thicket, the PRU pointman dropped to his knee to listen. He motioned me up beside him and pointed in the direction of the Cambodian outpost. I pointed in that direction as well and motioned for him to move out. The rest of the unit was spaced three to four meters apart as we moved into the open toward the Cambodian border.

The going was pretty easy considering we were in some fairly wet country. The mosquitoes were the only noise I could hear, other than the ever-so-slight sound of clothing brushing against a man's body as he slowly moved. We paused often to listen for any warning signs since we were definitely in no man's land.

The pointman froze as a flare from the outpost lit up our position. Two hours had passed since we left the river and we were now only about 300 meters from the small mud fort.

Our PRU pointman knew exactly where he was. Since I started using PRUs who were raised in the area where we were to operate, we had much better luck moving around populated areas. Our guide this night had family in this area of Cambodia and he knew the region especially well.

Remembering what Mr. Ward said to me, I often wondered, while operating alone with them, how much they actually knew about what was going on. Many of my troops were former Viet Cong and knew the value placed on a PRU; and an American PRU leader would be a pretty big score. To counter that, a bonus was paid to the PRUs who accompanied me on operations.

Another practice was to plan at least two operations to be run at the same time. Only just before the operation would the PRU know which one I was going on.

Since I had three ethnic groups to work with, I also encouraged each of them to "watch out" for the other. It wasn't paranoia that dictated this, just good practice for the business we were in. Tonight wasn't a problem since I wasn't exactly alone with a SEAL platoon with me. We had moved almost three kilometers so far, stopping occasionally to use the SEALs' starlight scope to check our route for enemy activity. We didn't have much natural light for the scope but occasionally a flare would go off from the Cambodian position to provide artificial starlight that worked just as well.

The trail we were on was heavily worn and no doubt frequented by the locals. I knew that we were getting close to the Cambodian outpost and was glad that the group was moving so quietly.

The only sound I could hear from our element was a few hushed words regarding Silver. One of the SEALs became agitated that the dog was acting strangely and was nervous. As we neared the outpost, Silver alerted and resisted attempts to be controlled and tried to lunge past me.

The pointman froze just as three rounds of small-arms fire whizzed past our heads. "Down," I whispered, and the pointman raced back to my position. "Hold your fire," I cautioned. "They may be just reconning by fire. Dick, bring the radio up. I want to see if I can reach An Phu and see if the U.S. advisor is in camp. If he is, we may be able to get some 155mm artillery support if we need it. Right now we hold it until we can confirm the size of the unit that's up there."

By this time the small-arms fire was sporadic and seemed to be just what I thought, recon by fire, a tactic used by both sides to get the other side to give away their position by returning fire. We weren't going to fall for that trap.

Looking back on that event, I know that Silver could smell and hear the enemy and was totally tuned in with his senses. He probably slowed us down enough to avoid being ambushed or hit booby traps that the PRU and I knew were in the area. Sure we were on a trail, but I was counting on the PRU to know the area well enough to avoid mines. After all he had a lot at stake since the pointman would more than likely step on the mine first!

The radio operator began moving up to my position, but stopped at Marcinko's side and told him that the skipper on one of the PBRs needed to talk with us ASAP. I thought that it must be important to break radio silence. As he handed the radio to Marcinko, I could see a bright light on the horizon in the direction of Chau Phu. Just then Marcinko hurried up to me saying, "Drew, there's a problem in Chau Doc."

"What kind of problem?" I whispered.

"I'm not sure yet," he said excitedly. "It sounds like Chau Doc may be under attack. The skipper relayed a message from Ringo, whoever that is, to you. Something about getting back to Chau Doc."

The SEALs had blocked my view to the rear, so I shifted to get a better look at the bright light I had just seen. As I moved down the column, I could see lights that definitely were in the direction of the city. The low clouds seemed to magnify the glow.

In the span of just a few seconds, the scenario of the past few days began to unfold. I didn't need to talk with Jim—Ringo—to figure out what was happening. Everything rapidly fell into place. The lack of enemy activity over the past few days and the recon by fire in an area where VC moved around like they owned the place were indications that the VC had moved to a new location. There wasn't any enemy activity because they were already where they wanted to be!

One of the SEALs suggested that maybe the bright lights were from fireworks for Tet.

Not likely, I thought, unless the fireworks got out of hand and are burning the town down. And besides, what about the message to get back?

Just then radio silence was broken again. I could tell that the skipper from the boats sounded more urgent. Chau Doc definitely was under attack.

"Let's get moving now," I said. "Dick, make the coordination with the PBRs for us to be picked up at the closest point from here to the river."

Without replying, Marcinko made contact with the boats. Then with total disregard for the enemy at our location we broke contact and began a hasty retreat to rendezvous with the boats. Even Silver was a bit nervous, looking over his shoulder toward the Cambodian outpost.

Compared to the slow going coming in, it took us a fraction of the time to make it back to the river. Now we needed the extraction to work as well as the insertion.

As we approached the riverbank, I could barely make out a faint red light that broke the otherwise black night. It flashed once and was answered by a similar response from our side of the river. Almost immediately I could hear the boats maneuvering out in the river a good half mile in the distance. Then I saw a red light flash once again from a point just a few hundred feet off to our front. These guys are good I thought. No doubt they had practiced this routine many times.

A PBR was fast approaching us, backing off just before it reached the bank. The skipper cut the throttle and the boat nosed in. Hoss yelled low for half to get on the first boat, then I could see the other PBR moving in to get the rest of us. I got on the second boat with my PRUs and was followed by Hoss and the rest of the extraction party.

As we pulled away from the bank everyone was breathing a bit easier. We all knew that we had risked discovery by moving so fast. What we didn't realize was that there probably wasn't any enemy in the area who wasn't already engaged. The contact we had just made was probably from the Cambodian outpost and not from the VC.

I moved to the pilot house. I needed to find out what was going on, and I needed to talk with Jim. I asked the skipper if he had radio contact with the Embassy House. He immediately handed me the radio, saying "Drew, it's for you."

"Westhaven this is Ringo," the radio cracked in the quiet.

"Roger, Ringo. This is Westhaven. Over."

"Look here, we have a problem in Chau Doc. The place is under heavy attack."

"Roger! Is the Embassy House under attack?" I asked.

"No, not at the moment but we can't get out. I talked with the B-Team and was told that the entire town is under enemy control."

"Roger. What about casualties?"

"None at the house. I'm not sure about the civilians." Jim was referring to the several United States Agency for International Development (USAID) civilians who were assigned throughout the city on various "do-gooder" projects in this so-called pacified province.

"Westhaven," Jim called, his voice showing an uncharacteristic waiver.

"Roger, Ringo, what is it?"

"I tried to get to the nurse's quarters and couldn't. I tried. I'm afraid that it doesn't look good. I'm told the enemy has that area under control and the nurse is probably KIA."

Jim said that he talked with her on the land line right after the attack began but hadn't heard from her since. Jim was referring to Maggie Frankot, a volunteer American nurse who both of us had learned to like. She was a neat person, 24 years old and nice looking. A little too idealistic, we thought, and a bit naive to the ways of war, but had a hell of a heart. She had just come from a Peace Corps assignment in Afghanistan.

"Roger, we'll get back ASAP," I said. "I'll give you a call in an hour. See if you can find out the situation as far as enemy control. We need to be able to land where we can do the most good."

"Roger, Westhaven, right now it doesn't look good to dock here. If you could you wouldn't be able to get out anyway."

"OK," I responded. "Just let us know. We should be on station in about an hour and a half to two hours. Westhaven out."

I asked the skipper to put his other radio on a frequency that I gave him. I wanted to be able to monitor the friendly units' situations as we proceeded down the river toward Chau Phu. Almost immediately we began to hear frantic calls for fire support and reinforcements from An Phu, a district headquarters north of Chau

Phu and within Chau Doc Province. It was apparent that the current offensive was province-wide. I called Dick to come over and monitor the radio traffic.

"What do you think?" I asked.

"Sounds like the shit has hit the fan."

"No shit,' I replied. "Well I think you have come to the right place for some action."

"Sounds like it," he said, looking a bit apprehensive at the prospects of getting into a major conventional ground battle. That's not something Navy SEALs have much experience with.

So much for the cease-fire I thought, as the small force plowed through the night toward Chau Doc and certain major combat.

A few minutes later Marcinko handed me the radio, saying that Jim was on the horn.

"This is Westhaven. Over," feeling relieved at hearing that Alabama accent booming over the radio. The Embassy House must still be intact.

"Roger, Westhaven. What is your position and ETA?"

"We are about 15 clicks out and should be at your location in less than an hour," looking toward the skipper for confirmation.

"The House is still intact but I still don't recommend you dock here."

"Roger. We still need a recommendation on the best place to put ashore."

"Westhaven, it looks like this offensive is country-wide. I couldn't get through to Can Tho, and Saigon is reporting VC units in the city and said we're on our own for now."

"OK! What is your recommendation on the best place to go ashore?"

"I really can't tell you where to land. The whole town is crawling with VC. I talked with the VNs (short for Vietnamese national) and they aren't much help."

"Roger, I'll get back to you in a few minutes and let you know our plan."

Jim responded, saying that Maggie was still unaccounted for. Obviously her situation was of major concern to him.

I talked over the situation with Marcinko and the PBR skipper. The situation was so chaotic that no one really had any input. It was agreed that whatever I came up with would be OK. They all knew that I was more familiar with the layout of the city and the friendly situation than anyone else.

My plan was being formulated as I spoke. We would land our two boats at the park near the Vietnamese Tactical Operations Center (TOC). The other two PBRs would provide supporting fire from the river. We would assemble as soon as we landed and move to the TOC just a few hundred meters from the shore.

Jim had indicated that he had radio communications with the TOC so I was counting on it being secure. The TOC was the headquarters for all of the Vietnamese military units in the province.

At the point where we would land, there was a small park 100 to 150 feet wide that ran along the river. It wouldn't provide much cover—in fact, it was pretty open. At least the PBRs could see us to provide covering fire with their .50s. I knew I was really reaching with that one. Both the SEALs and I felt a lot better in heavy brush. This operation was going to be a little like hitting the beach at Normandy!

Someone from the rear saw the humor and said, "Yeah, we won't have a lot of trees to get in the way when we're running, either." With that, everyone laughed. Each of us had his own way to deal with the unknown.

Marcinko asked about the idea of landing further out of town to the south.

I said that then we'd have to fight our way back into town, probably through fortified positions. The VC would certainly be expecting a counter-attack from either the south or the west and might be waiting for friendly ground reinforcements. Going into the heart of the city would give us an element of surprise since a Navy assault would be highly unlikely.

I thought to myself that the only weakness with my plan was the lack of intelligence on enemy positions. Where did they attack from and in what strength? If they had a unit that approached from the river, then they still could have their rear elements and reinforcements near the river. We'd be moving right into them.

Chau Phu was located where the Bassac came in from the east and the Chau Doc River came in from the north. The place where we were going to land was not far from this confluence. In the past, when the VC attacked B-42, the Special Forces B-Team Headquarters, they did so from across the Chau Doc River using the Chinese noodle factory as a rocket position.

Things were moving kind of fast and discussing all of these contingencies would only confuse the issue. Besides it was only a guess. If we planned for every contingency on this operation, we wouldn't have enough time to complete the mission. The situation was so bad that this time we needed just to get in there and take care of business.

One other thing I said to the skipper and Marcinko, "We're going in right at BMNT (beginning morning nautical twilight, a time just before light that allows about 400 meters of visibility). This will give us some cover of darkness for the boats. We need to be able to get in without the enemy's crew-served weapons being able to fire on us as we approach the city. It also will give those of us on the ground the necessary daylight to be seen by the friendlies defending the TOC. No doubt the VNs will be a little trigger happy by now."

Hoss and Marcinko went to each of their men and briefed them on the upcoming operation and then called the other boat and briefly outlined the plan with the other half of the platoon.

As I went to my PRUs to do the same, I could hear the skipper going over the plan with the other boats. This time I wished I had brought a Vietnamese PRU. It was going to be tough convincing the friendlies at the TOC that my Cambodes weren't VC. After all they dressed like VC and couldn't speak much Vietnamese either. I'd have to be our point. This time it was going to be better for a roundeye to make the first contact.

The skipper of the lead boat slowed down so we wouldn't arrive too early. As a result our progress was painfully slow. Everyone, I'm sure, could sense the anxiety building for the upcoming assault.

# CHAPTER 3

## A LITTLE LIKE NORMANDY

We rounded the last bend as the boats approached the confluence of the two rivers. We were about 1500 meters (just under a mile) from the beach and I could see that the entire city appeared to be engulfed in flames or smoke.

The sound that comes from a mortar round being dropped into the tube by enemy gunners could be easily heard among the explosions of rockets and high-explosive ordinance going off. It appeared that the pop and the thump sounds of the rounds being dropped in the tubes were coming from within the city. The explosions would appear just a short distance away, indicating to me that the VC mortars were already in the city.

More than likely the attack originated from within the city as well. I could see a hell of a lot of tracers, both red and green. The bright green tracers of the VC clearly outnumbered the meager answer of red.

The four boats were staggered in a column. It wasn't difficult for the .50 gunners to pick out a section of beach to engage. I pointed to the beach where we were to land and the skipper ordered his gunners to fire in that direction. Seeing this, the first boat in our column began raking the beach with its .50s and all of the others joined in taking a section of the shore under fire.

The confluence of the two rivers gave the boats plenty of shore to engage. All four of the boats were now at top speed approaching 25 knots. The big diesels of the MK IIs roared as they closed in on the objective. The lead boat veered off to the south as the next two with us on them, moved toward shore.

Rocket fire could be seen as the enemy realized we were there. Off to our right I could see water geysers as mortar rounds dropped into the water. Green tracers from the machine-gun fire raced by, and cracking sounds overhead could be detected as several individual enemy riflemen joined in firing on the PBRs.

So far it looked like we just might make it without any casualties. The .50-calibers were extremely effective and seemed to cause the enemy gunners close to the shore to let up enough to give us an edge just as the two boats nosed onto the beach simultaneously.

The city appeared much as a glowing and turbulent storm as I leaped from the bow. The entire force was off the boats in five or six seconds. As the last man was in mid-stride of his jump, the boat lurched in reverse and was off to join the others in the middle of the river.

The PBRs, now back in a staggered column, were concentrating their fire along our side of the river. Huge limbs were falling from the trees in the park as the heavy .50-caliber bullets sheared them off. The hollow "thunk" sounds were clearly audible as the rounds struck the solid tree trunks.

I yelled over the noise as did some of the others. "Is everyone

OK?" Several sounded together that all were all right. I could even pick out the voices of the Cambodes as they made an attempt at an OK in English.

"Let's move out," I yelled, and advanced. I needed to be the first at the TOC. Maybe someone would recognize me. No doubt the defenders would know something was up. The PBRs would hardly go unnoticed, especially seeing the .50s rounds striking the walls of the TOC headquarters.

"Call the boats and get them to shift their fire to the south and to the north of the point we landed," I yelled. "They are hitting friendly positions."

"Roger," said the radio operator. I could hear the skipper acknowledge the command.

The fire immediately shifted toward the Chau Doc hospital, which was located across the road from the river and on the same side of the road we were now on. It looked as if the enemy had decided to use that major structure as a stronghold. In any case, the PBRs had that under control and were directing an unrelenting volume of fire on the building as they made their pass.

Racing across the street, I yelled for the rest of the group to hold their position until contact was made with the TOC. I rushed the entrance as a sentry spotted me and yelled something in Vietnamese. "OK," I yelled, hoping that he would recognize this as it was the most notable American phrase I could think of.

He did, but seemed to want to hold a conversation with me and was reluctant to open the gate.

"God damn it," I yelled. "You dien dau son of a bitch."

He understood my tone of voice as did his sergeant who rushed out to help, looking me over thinking that I was wounded.

Seeing me enter the compound, the SEALs followed me in. I hadn't noticed until I entered that my PRUs were right on my heels when I first rushed the compound. We no doubt looked like a pretty aggressive bunch as we rushed into the small courtyard.

All eyes were on us. They looked confused, not knowing for sure whether we were their saviors or their enemy! Once it became apparent that we were on their side, they swarmed over us as if we had rescued them from certain death. Little did they know that we were just one rung up the ladder of safety from where they were and the top of that ladder was not yet in sight.

I was moving through the small band of defenders trying to find someone who knew what was going on and spoke English. The SEALs were huddled around a group of Vietnamese soldiers who were passing out food. My PRUs were enjoying somewhat celebrity status as they were questioned by some Vietnamese officers.

I spotted the familiar face of Major Phoung, the acting province chief, sitting with his back against the nearest building. I knew him to be an aggressive soldier and one who knew what was going on. He spoke excellent English and would be a welcome source of information.

Approaching him, I could see that something wasn't quite right. "Thieu ta, (Major) Phoung," I called out. "What is the situation?"

Hearing no response, I yelled out, "Major Phoung, tell me what is going on? Where are the enemy positions and what is the friendly situation?"

Again hearing no response I moved closer. One of his officers stepped between us as I reached down to grab the major.

"Get back, God damn it," I ordered. "We're here to help out and I need some answers."

The loyal officer jumped back, not wanting a confrontation. No doubt he was trying to save embarrassment for his commander but thought better of interfering.

Through the lieutenant's broken English, I was able to make out that the VC had occupied the city just after midnight. One of the first places they attacked was Major Phoung's house, probably with hopes of capturing him. It seemed that the major wasn't home, lucky for him. But the VC, upon entering his compound, apparently killed his family and his bodyguard. The bodyguard and a few others must have put up a hell of a fight before they lost the compound. The loss of his family and bodyguard was too much for Major Phoung to handle.

After hearing this, I went back over to where the major was sitting.

"Major," I said, a bit more sympathetic, "you've got to get your troops together. They are counting on you. We've got to get your city back."

He looked pathetic, just sitting against the wall of that building with his legs stretched out as if he had slid down the wall in that position and wasn't going to move.

"Major, look at me," I pleaded. "We don't know what's happened to your family. Maybe they will keep them alive to bargain with."

Hearing this he made his first response: "Drew, they killed my wife and two children and my good friend too."

"I know that's what it looks like but we can't be sure," I replied. I was trying to give him a little hope.

"The VC take everything," he said. "We must leave."

"No," I said, "we must not leave. We must go into the city and find out what the situation is. How many soldiers do you have?"

"Not many," he told me. "Most of them are on leave for the New Year."

"Did they leave the city or did they stay here?"

"About half went away."

"So how many of your soldiers are in the city somewhere?"

At that point, the officer I previously confronted piped up that there are about 50 here in the compound and another 100 on leave in the city. Not a very large force, I thought, to take the city back. Right then it didn't look like Major Phoung was going to release any of the 50 holed up here in the TOC.

"We must go, Major Phoung," I told him. "I must go to the Embassy House and check that out. I need to see how Jim Moore and Westall are doing."

"You can't go. You must stay here, Drew, and help protect the city from here." His voice cracked as he spoke.

"No, we're going to the Embassy House."

Not saying a word or even looking up, he settled back down to his resting place. No doubt he thought his world was over.

I found Marcinko talking with his men.

"Look, guys," I said as I walked up, "I'm going to the Embassy House. I've got to get back and check things out. I'll take the PRUs with me."

"Why don't you take a couple of my guys with you," replied Marcinko. I thought I could use the company. "Harry go with him . . ." and before Marcinko could finish, Frank Thornton volunteered to go along.

"See if one of the PBRs can pick us up near where they dropped us off" I suggested. "That would save us a little time. They could drop us off at the docks at the house."

"Right," Marcinko said. "I'll give them a call and see if they can handle that."

The enemy fire at that point had dropped off significantly since it was obvious that there wasn't much friendly resistance and the enemy forces were consolidating their positions.

The five of us dashed out of the gates and headed for the beach as we saw the PBR swing toward us as it deviated from one of its passes. We reached the boat just as it reached the beach. The fire was not nearly as heavy as when we arrived earlier that morning but was still a concern.

No doubt the fire from a dozen .50-calibers had gotten their attention and they didn't want to engage the PBRs for no real reason. The skipper didn't waste any time in backing off the beach. It almost seemed like the recoil from the .50s helped propel the boat backwards. As we headed for the Embassy House, the remaining three boats laid down an effective screen of steel. I have to admit, I felt proud to be a part of that team.

As the hospital came into view I could see enemy snipers popping their heads out of the upper floor windows and firing on the boats as we raced by. They have balls, I thought. The .50-caliber rounds can punch through the concrete in those buildings like it was made of cardboard.

The main street that paralleled the river was virtually blocked with tree limbs knocked down by the .50-caliber fire. I made a mental note of that as the hospital was left in our wake. We must have been doing 30 knots as we approached the Embassy House. The trip lasted three or four minutes. The boat that carried us didn't cut power until we were less than 100 meters from the docks.

I could see two of the Nungs on the docks run up the stairs as we approached, thinking that we weren't going to be able to stop in time before we hit the docks. The wake from the boat set the small docks into a wild bucking frenzy. The five of us jumped down as several of the Nungs ran down to secure the ropes holding the dock in place.

"Hey, Nago, where's Jim?"

Nago pointed to the radio room. As I ran to see Jim, I called to Nago to get my Jeep ready and load extra boxes of .50-caliber ammo on it. "Yes, sir," he responded as he started calling out instructions to the Nungs.

I walked in just as Jim was putting the radio down.

"Good to see you, Drew."

"Yeah, Jim, good to be back. What's up?"

As Jim stood, he pulled a cigar out of his sleeve: "I talked with Colonel Smith at B-42 and he said from his position, it looked like the VC had complete control of the city. He said the VC appeared to be moving around freely, just like they owned the place."

"I guess that means the civilians are in enemy control (referring to the U.S. civilians) and Maggie too."

"Yeah, Drew, I tried to get to her."

"OK, Jim, I'm planning to go to the TOC and get the rest of the SEALs and go see what's going on and figure out what we can do about it."

"I'm going too," Jim said, just as Westy came in.

"I'm going too," Westy said. "I've got the Nungs putting the A-6 machine gun on the pedestal in my Jeep."

"OK," I told them. "We've got to leave in 15 minutes."

"We'll be ready," Jim replied.

Nago came running in, saying that the two Jeeps were ready and gassed as well.

"Nago can go?" he asked.

"OK, Nago, you can go. You go with Westall."

The two Jeeps were still behind the safety of the compound walls. My gold Willys Jeep was parked in front with Westy's blue one waiting behind. The two vehicles looked rather formidable. They would have to be, I thought, to do what we needed.

Jim climbed into the right seat as I said, "The suicide seat is yours." He laughed for the first time since we made it back. Frank climbed up and claimed the .50. Harry stood to the side and took up position as assistant gunner. He hefted an arm full of linked .50-caliber rounds and said, "I'm ready."

Westy climbed behind the wheel of his Jeep and Nago stood

behind him on the .30-caliber A-6 machine-gun. I ran to my room and retrieved a PRC-25 radio which I thought would come in handy. I tossed it between the seats of my Jeep along with spare batteries and climbed in.

"Let's go," I yelled. Vinh pushed both halves of the heavy steel gates open, smiled a concerned smile and gave a sharp thumb's up.

# CHAPTER 4

## LET'S GO
## TO MAGGIE'S

I floored the accelerator and the Jeep roared through the gate. Making an immediate right turn, the Jeep leaned on two wheels. Frank and Harry collided as the heavy gun swung on its pedestal.

"Take it easy, save us for the fight," Harry yelled as he and Frank hefted the big gun back around.

"You guys OK?" Jim yelled as he held on.

Everyone was all business but the adrenaline rush overpowered any fear we had. In two or three minutes, we would be in front of the hospital and then all hell would break loose. As the hospital came into view, it confirmed my worst fears. Tree limbs that had been knocked off by the PBRs .50s completely blocked the road. With no way around, I said we're going through.

"Give 'em hell." Frank yelled as he let loose a long burst with the .50. I swerved to hit the smallest part of a huge tree branch that was lying across the road. As I swerved, Frank and the heavy .50 swung to a 90-degree angle. He managed to hang on, not missing a beat with his steady rate of fire.

I felt the Jeep leave the ground as we passed over the tree. Harry managed to hang on as well and expertly fed the belt to the gun. As the gun swung over my head, I felt each round going off. The concussion of the gun shattered the windshield and the rearview mirror on my side of the Jeep.

The enemy were caught by surprise and only managed to get off 30 or 40 rounds of AK-47 fire. Even so it amazed me that no one was hit, considering the enemy were firing from concealed positions only 20 to 30 yards away. As we raced by, I could see enemy snipers hanging out of the windows to get a better shot at us. Tracers were hitting the tree branches just to the front of our vehicle.

I could hear the little .30-caliber on Westy's Jeep behind us pouring out steady six- to eight-round bursts. Without looking back, I pressed on. Jim yelled that they made it by. "Great," I told him. "Keep your eyes on the building ahead."

Frank was already on it, selectively firing at any likely window that could have a sniper in it.

Approaching the TOC, the sniper fire began dropping off. There is a tendency, I thought, to call all enemy fire in built-up areas like a city sniper fire. In actuality they were enemy units positioned in buildings hidden from view. Snipers generally are stationary, making maximum use of concealment. These soldiers were highly mobile infantry units, moving around the city much as a squad or platoon would do in the jungle. The main difference was that these units were using buildings and walls instead of trees and other foliage.

Also, they had opened up interior and exterior walls so they could move inside from room to room and building to building within the city blocks rather than being out on the streets like we were. This became obvious to me since I hadn't seen any groups of enemy moving down the streets. I also observed this tactic used on a much smaller scale by the rebel forces in Santo Domingo while assigned with the 82nd Airborne Division in 1965. It was very effective and was extremely difficult to counter unless you knew it. I was thinking that we'd have to figure their network somehow if we were going to get them out of town.

As the Jeep raced up to the TOC, the large metal gates swung open as if I had pushed a button. After both vehicles were safely inside, the two guards quickly closed them.

The SEALs who remained at the TOC hurried over and all seemed anxious to find out what was going on, as if we had a lot of information.

Marcinko walked up and asked, "What's the plan, guys?"

For a minute I waited for someone to respond. Finally I said, "The first thing we have to do is find out what's happened to Maggie."

Marcinko responded, saying that he was able to talk with Major Phoung, who said Maggie and the others probably were dead like his wife.

Jim joined me in saying that was bullshit.

"We're going to find out one way or the other," I said forcefully. "Anyway, we have to go over in that direction to see what's going on. Let's go to Maggie's."

Jim responded with a loud "Let's go!" Harry and Frank climbed up onto my Jeep. Jim returned to the "suicide seat" and settled in. Upon seeing the two Jeeps wheeling around, the TOC gate automatically swung open. No sooner had we cleared the gate, than I was in third gear with Westy in close pursuit.

Upon making the first turn toward Maggie's house we immediately began receiving a high volume of enemy fire coming from several of the taller buildings on both sides of the street. Frank and

Harry appeared to be trading positions as the heavy gun whirled back and forth. As I saw it, Harry and Frank were taking turns firing as the gun came into their hands. In any case they were doing a great job handling the situation. When one fired, the other kept the gun supplied with ammunition.

When we rounded the last corner and Maggie's house came into view, my first thought was that we were too late. I could see her International Scout sitting directly in front of her house. It was riddled with bullet holes. There were no less than a thousand holes in it. It was listing at an angle. All but one tire had been shot out. No glass was intact and the windshield molding was lying on the hood.

It was obvious the others were thinking the same thing by the disappointed looks on their faces. These thoughts quickly vanished as the rate of enemy fire quickly escalated to a steady volume.

The one thing that caught my attention was that one VC apparently was armed with an M-79 grenade launcher. I could hear the hollow "tink" sound the weapon made when it was first fired. Then came the unmistakable blast of the high-explosive round going off. This weapon was very effective and I really didn't want to be on the receiving end of it.

Major Phoung's bodyguard was always seen with one and this one might well have been his. It was further evidence that Major Phoung was right. His bodyguard most likely was dead. It didn't look good for his wife and children either, I thought.

The courtyard at Maggie's house looked like a hurricane had hit it. Most of the leaves of the many trees in her front yard were on the ground and patio. Her house also was riddled with bullet holes and had evidence that it had been hit by B-40 rocket fire.

Sliding the Jeep to a stop, I saw two VC run from the courtyard and duck around toward the back of the house. As Jim and I ran up to the front door, I called for someone to watch the side of the house.

The last thing we needed was for those two to pop back around and hose us down while we were busy trying to get Maggie out. Somebody responded with a loud "Gotcha covered."

Jim and I crossed the open area between the street and the house. As we approached we could see that the front door was open but the iron gate was closed. Maggie's house, as did many of the other permanent structures in Chau Phu, had heavy iron gates and bars over the windows. I looked through the gate as we approached and could see a half dozen VC running from the front room into the kitchen. They darted through a hole in the back of the house which they had prepared for that purpose.

This, as I said earlier, allowed the enemy easy access to other buildings without having to use the streets. During this time the enemy fire had not dropped off and I was grateful for whoever was on the .50-caliber machine gun. If it had not been for the fifty, the enemy may have been able to maneuver on us.

Both Jim and I were on our knees as I tried the iron gate. No luck, it was locked. I yelled this out as Jim called in. "Maggie," he yelled, "Maggie, it's Jim!" There was no answer.

I ran to the side of the building to make sure the six VC we saw going through the back wall weren't coming around the house. I ran back to Jim, crouched down and told him, "I'm going to try to shoot the lock open."

As I stood up to do just that, I heard a faint female voice coming from a rear room in the corner of the house. Jim and I exchanged glances as I said, "It sounds like Maggie."

Jim and I both called her name again. "Maggie, it's Drew. Where are you?"

"I'm here," she replied softly.

"Come to the front door," I called out.

"The VC are in here," she told us.

"No, Maggie," I said. "They're gone. Open the door and come out."

Just as Maggie opened the door of her hiding place, two more VC ran to the rear of the house, barely missing her. It happened so fast that none of us could react, including the VC. They must have been hiding in another room and decided to make a break for it.

Maggie ducked back as the two VC passed her. Now we knew where she was but still couldn't get to her. Jim and I were down on our knees, exchanging glances, looking for an idea. Suddenly she emerged again from the corner room and slowly made her way toward us.

She was wading through a three-foot-high pile of furniture and trash the VC had left there after going through it, no doubt looking for anything of value. I stood up and tried the gate again. No luck, and Maggie reached out to help with the gate. Standing there, I was feeling very helpless. Just inches away and not able to get to her.

The enemy were no doubt in the next building and I thought I could hear them talking. We had to get moving. Soon they would figure out that we weren't a really large force and they certainly would attack us. I doubted if we would be able to hold out for very long and we couldn't count on our Vietnamese allies. At least, not for awhile anyway.

"Maggie," I said, as I reached for her hand, "do you know where the key is?"

I didn't realize until much later how stupid that must have sounded. She didn't hesitate and turned to that pile of trash in the middle of the floor. She rummaged around and in no time came up with the key. She clutched it to her as she ran toward us. Her hands trembling, she tried to put it into the lock from the inside. I reached in through the bars to steady her hand. I knew we only had seconds to spare. We were really exposed to fire from across the street.

Rounds were smacking the front of the building where Jim and I were standing. The lock finally opened, but the gate was badly bent. As I struggled to open it, Jim stood up and helped me pull it back enough so that I was able to pull Maggie through. I pushed her down for additional protection and she tripped over the threshold of the metal gate, injuring her knee.

We ran at a crouch and both Jim and I half carried her to the second Jeep. We made good time, I'm sure, but it seemed to take us forever to cover the 30 or so feet to the street. I helped her into Westy's Jeep and laid her down in the tiny rear cargo area. Everyone moved from their firing positions and climbed aboard.

It was customary to put flak jackets on the seats of vehicles for the obvious reason in case of hitting mines. We had them on ours and the SEALs covered Maggie with the four we had on our seats. Harry left his .50 to somebody else and piled into Westy's Jeep.

I wheeled the Jeep around in a half-circle and stopped. I yelled to Westy to pull around and head to the TOC: "We'll cover you!"

The dust and gravel from Westy's Jeep showered us as he sped by. As soon as he straightened out we turned to follow. As we departed, the enemy fire intensified. No doubt we had been pushing our luck. We had been at Maggie's house for more than seven or eight minutes, which is a damn long time to be stationary in a fast moving-scenario like we had going here.

We made it to the TOC in less than two minutes. Again, the two gates swung open as if they were automatic. As we cleared the street, the remaining SEALs rushed to our sides. All were visibly happy that we had been successful and Maggie was OK.

Doc Nixon rushed over and examined Maggie's knee as she protested. "It's OK," she said as he tried to put a dressing on it. He helped her to the nearest building and eased her down on the porch and began to tend to her again, with Maggie still resisting.

"Doc," I said, "you can take care of that when we get back to the Embassy House. We need to go now and you two can go with us. I'm not sure how long this place will last (referring to the TOC). The VC may try to take it."

"I agree," Jim responded. "We should move back there as soon as possible. Yeah, Jim, and now is probably the best time to go. The PBRs seem to be getting a handle on the hospital. They should be able to give us fire support as we move down the street in front of the hospital."

Someone said he heard the Vietnamese talking about some Americans holed up at their quarters. Jim said that he heard from Mr. Flashpoler (the senior USAID advisor and acting senior provincial advisor) by radio that there were eight civilians in the group and that they were surrounded but OK.

"All right then," I responded, "we'll get them after we take Maggie back to the house and re-supply with ammo. Who is going with me to the Embassy House?"

As expected, Harry and Frank were the first to volunteer. Then Schwalenberg and Risher quickly responded, Risher saying, "Let's get to it." Risher climbed into my Jeep. Harry claimed the .50 this time. Schwalenberg armed with the Stoner, also assumed position as assistant gunner. Doc and Maggie loaded onto Westy's vehicle as did Frank. The gate again swung open and the Vietnamese guard saluted as we raced through.

We turned right this time and headed for the gauntlet one more time. As the hospital came into view, I couldn't help but think we were beginning to push our luck. As we got nearer, I could see the PBRs beginning to make their firing run. We would make our approach in time with theirs and hopefully get by.

As all four boats commenced firing, we accelerated and were approaching 50 miles an hour as we hit the downed trees. The PBRs, upon seeing us, shifted their fire as we approached.

By this time the pathway was easy to find and we easily jumped through. Each time we did, I held my breath hoping the shocks wouldn't give out. After all, my Jeep was carrying an extremely heavy load. There were four fairly heavy guys each with their basic load of combat gear and then there was the weight of the .50 and its ammo. This was putting a lot of stress on the frame.

As we approached the Embassy House, we only received sporadic fire. It looked as if the Viet Cong were saving our headquarters for last. I could see Sieu and Lin on top of the bunker watching as we approached. Not leaving their position, they yelled for someone to open the gates. I pulled in as far as I could so Westy would have room to squeeze in behind me. The compound was not built to accommodate two vehicles but we managed.

I told Nago, as he was climbing down from behind the .30-caliber on Westy's Jeep, to get more ammo for the .50 and whatever he needed.

"Yes, sir," he said, as he set out to finish his task.

Some of the Nungs passed out small loaves of not-so-warm French bread that had been partially broken open and filled with scrambled duck eggs. I hadn't developed a fondness of duck eggs, as they were so rich. I have to admit though, they tasted pretty damn good this time. With the exception of a few bites of Navy C-rations, aboard the PBRs, I hadn't eaten for more than 24 hours.

Jim said that he needed to stay at the Embassy House to coordinate the PBR support and try to find out what was happening in Can Tho, which was our regional headquarters.

"Right," I said. "Eventually the allies will get their shit together and respond with some kind of counter-attack."

"Yeah," Jim replied, "but I doubt if it'll be anytime soon. It looks like this offensive is more than a show of force. I wish we could get hold of some heavy hitter (referring to a high-ranking member of the VC infrastructure)."

"Right Jim, I'll put an order in for one."

Jim was right though, we needed a break like that if we were to find out what their intentions were. But first we had to get the rest of the civilians out.

I needed to look over my Jeep. It had been put through a lot and would need to do a lot more before this battle was over. I met Nago on the way carrying two cans of .50-caliber ammo.

"Fifty good," he said as he heaved them on board.

"Yeah, Nago, the .50 is 'numba one,'" as I gave him a thumbs up. Nago was proud of his service with the Americans. He was a good soldier and knew weapons extremely well.

Nago learned to like the Special Forces, first starting out at the age of 16 with a Special Forces A-Team and later with the Special Forces Mike Force. The Mike Force units probably saw more combat than any unit in Vietnam. Formed early in the war, they had the mission to reinforce Special Forces A-Camps already under attack throughout the country. These camps, usually manned by a 12-man Special Forces team advising anywhere from 500 to 1,500 indigenous troops, were located in some of the most remote and strategically important real estate in the country.

As a result, they were often attacked, usually in bad weather when conventional air support was not able to fly. It was commonly thought that the enemy could overrun most any A-Team it chose if they were willing to pay the price. The Mike Force units were led by some pretty tough and aggressive Special Forces types. So the Mike Force was almost always deployed into a hot situation.

Each unit was formed following strict ethnic guidelines. Some were all Vietnamese, some were all Cambodian and some like Nago's were totally Chinese Nungs, whom I thought were the most aggressive. For this reason they often suffered extraordinary casualties. That was not due to any lack of skill or effectiveness but by the pure fact they were often put into impossible situations.

As a result, the Nung leadership was discouraging Nung units larger than platoon-size. The reason was simply to try to preserve the future generations of their culture. So to our good fortune, Nago and the other Nungs were available for this job as embassy security. There wasn't anything that Nago wouldn't do for us.

I also felt that he kind of liked me and this made me especially proud. I hoped that we would be able to sit down after this was over and have a couple of beers. He was great to talk with because he was so matter of fact and extremely realistic. What you saw was what you got.

Jim came up to me while I was trying to repair the footrest that was fabricated to the rear bumper of my Jeep. The .50 was so long that the gunner had to stand out on this platform. It had started to come loose due to extra use it had been getting jumping over the trees in front of the hospital. Seeing that it wasn't going to work, I told two of the Nungs to take it off. The .50 crew would have to try to fit inside. Right now that was small stuff and didn't really matter in the big picture.

"Drew," Jim said, "I'd like to call in one of the PBRs to get Maggie out. How long will it be before you can get to the other civilians?"

"We'll be leaving in a few minutes," I told him. "We should know something soon."

"OK, I'll wait until I hear from you then."

"Sounds good, Jim."

"Westy is going to stay here too."

"OK," I yelled for someone to drive Westy's Jeep. "Let's get going!"

# CHAPTER 5

## RUNNING THE GAUNTLET

We quickly loaded up and Vinh opened the double gates for us. I wheeled around toward the hospital. This time I drove a little slower so I wouldn't lose Harry Humphries.

"Thanks, Drew," he snickered, always on the alert to make something humorous out of a bad situation. I was glad to see that Harry hadn't lost his sense of humor.

We approached the hospital for what seemed to be the hundredth time, but in reality it was only the third. As before, we hit the trees at full speed. This time we didn't receive any enemy fire. That didn't cause Harry and whoever was on the little .30 behind us to hold back. They were giving them hell. Even though I couldn't tell if we were receiving any fire from the bad guys, I could see figures dashing back and forth between the upper-floor windows.

I yelled as we passed that we were going straight to the civilians' compound. I knew right where it was and thought that now was as good a time as any and we didn't need anything at the TOC. We cruised right by the TOC and could see our "automatic" gate start to open, no doubt thinking we were coming in.

I've always been confident that I could avoid setting a pattern. To do so would mean certain death in my business. I shuddered upon seeing the friendlies anticipating our next move. The VC were no dummies and would be looking for this kind of weakness. I'd have to do something about it, I thought.

As soon as we made the first turn past the TOC, I could see the tail-end of several individuals dashing into an alley. They quickly disappeared and we began to receive heavy fire from that direction almost immediately. Out of the corner of my eye I could see figures dashing back and forth between windows in the upper stories of the taller buildings.

Rounds were hitting the street to our front and Harry took the enemy positions under fire. He was swinging the gun back and forth as if responding to each position as they opened up. I could feel the small gold Jeep recoil from each two- to three-round burst.

Harry didn't let up until we made the next turn down a narrow street that led to the pre-fab buildings that housed the civilians. For a few moments it seemed like a lull just before a storm. The fire dropped off just as suddenly as it had started. It was almost too quiet, I thought.

Just then two B-40 rockets crossed near us and hit a building to our front. The VC tried to get us into an ambush but acted a little too prematurely. They had a good plan to catch us in a rocket ambush, but to our good fortune their execution lacked discipline. No doubt they knew we were going to try to reach the civilians.

The .50 responded in the direction of the suspected gunners. I proceeded another 60 yards and could see through the small gate of the compound that one of the pre-fab buildings was to the ground, although it was still smoking.

A few rounds popped over our heads. I slid the Jeep to a halt just past the entrance to the compound. Grabbing my Swedish-K, I exited the vehicle before it came to a complete halt. I looked back and could see Harry swinging on the end of the .50. He was completely outside the vehicle and not about to let go of the gun. The momentum of my sudden stop carried him all the way around to the front of the Jeep.

Still firing, he was really cussing. "Jesus Christ," he yelled. The rate of fire he was putting out seemed to do the trick. The VC kept their heads down and the small-arms fire practically stopped.

"OK guys," I yelled, "I'm going into the compound. You three cover us from the right and you two to the left. Keep the .50 going."

I ran directly for the burned-out structure. I wasn't sure what I expected to find. Maybe there would be just a few bodies. I hoped not. At least we would know if they were alive or not.

I could see two VC firing over the back wall of the compound as I entered. They were only about 25 yards behind the destroyed pre-fab building directly to my front. I ran forward and fired a burst from my Swedish-K toward the VC on the back wall. They ducked down and didn't show their faces again.

B-40 rocket rounds were going off to my right. I couldn't tell whether any small-arms fire was coming from the entrance to the compound I had just left. I hoped the guys behind me were all right. Rocket fire continued but seemed to be coming from a greater distance and not a factor just yet. I still wondered whether the rockets were making hits or not but I couldn't afford to look back to see.

I could hear the .50 continuing it's two- and three-round bursts. That gun is very impressive in city combat. There really isn't a safe place for the enemy to go. The heavy .50-caliber rounds punched right through the old cement and mortar.

They must be OK, I thought, as I ran toward the rear of the compound and continued to look around for any evidence that the civilians were in the area. I rushed from one concealed area to another, still not knowing what I might find. I passed the second pre-fab structure. It looked like it had taken a direct hit and was destroyed but had not burned. It appeared to have been ransacked by enemy ground units that had been through here after the buildings were hit and were searching for things they could use. That was probably them I saw going over the back wall.

As I passed a bunker in the corner, I heard an American voice. I looked around and I saw a familiar dark face. It was the agriculture advisor I met a few days earlier in Chau Doc in what was beginning to seem like another life.

"Drew," he called out. "We are in here."

"How many of you are there?"

He said, "We're all here, all eight of us."

"Shit hot!" I yelled. "All right, let's go. I've got two Jeeps over there and some guys waiting to take you back."

"No! We can't come out, the Viet Cong are still here." He obviously felt more secure in the bunker and didn't want to leave the safety of it.

I could actually feel the rounds as they snapped by me. Dropping to one knee to continue the conversation, I couldn't blame him but I knew the situation could change fast.

"No, damn it! You're coming out now or we're going without you. The VC aren't here now but they are on their way back. We've got to go now."

On hearing that, he ducked his head back into his hiding place and motioned to the others and said very forcefully, "Let's go. Drew wants us to go now."

All eight lucky souls dutifully filed out. I yelled for them to get down and follow me, which they did. Again, dropping to one knee, I motioned for them to head for the gate, while keeping a watch toward the back wall. They all instinctively bent over and hurried past me in a single file toward the main entrance to where the SEALs and Nago were waiting about 30 meters away.

Nago and the SEALs automatically pulled back from their covering positions as the party reached them.

I could hear the grateful civilians, obviously overjoyed with being rescued. They were jumping around like young school children. I couldn't believe what was going on. Some of them actually were trying to shake hands with Nago. They are really a naive bunch. They actually think they've been saved. I wondered how many of them were coming back after this is over when they realized just how lucky they were.

"You people aren't safe until you get out of this place," I shouted. "All of you get your asses into that Jeep."

Nago and one SEAL accompanied them. The four of us who remained climbed into my Jeep. It might have seemed more practical to divide the load but who said we had to be practical. My vehicle had to be maneuverable so we could provide covering fire on the way back to the TOC.

It was almost comical as Westy's Jeep sagged under the load of those 10 people on board. The under-carriage scraped and groaned as it began slowly to pick up speed.

I yelled, "Let's go to the TOC!"

I could hear the SEALS let out profanities as our force "raced" out like turtles. Now we needed some luck. We'd be sitting ducks for enemy gunners. Hopefully Harry would be able to silence them as he did when we came in earlier.

Whatever the reason, the VC didn't attack us on the way to the TOC. The trip this time was uneventful as we limped back. We made the turn into the TOC compound and the Vietnamese all cheered as they saw this comical sight. We pulled in and would stay just long enough to tell the remaining SEALs that we were going to take the civilians straight to the Embassy House.

The situation at the TOC hadn't changed much. The few defenders were scampering around yelling in excited high-pitched voices. Each time a sniper round would hit the compound, all would duck and then a small swarm would scurry like crabs to a corner of the compound and fire back. This ritual kept up the whole time we were there. They still hadn't gotten their act together.

This place was getting a little scary, I thought. The VC are missing a prime opportunity if they don't attack now.

I picked up my PRC-25 radio and called Jim at the house.

"Ringo, this is Westhaven, over."

"Roger, Westhaven, Ringo is down at the docks talking with one of the PBR crews." I recognized Westy's voice.

"Roger, give him a message that all civilians are accounted for and we will be there in 15 minutes. Also call the PBRs and tell them we'd like some covering fire as we head back."

"Roger. Good work. Are there any injuries? Over."

"Negative, they're all in good shape. Westhaven out."

Major Phoung, upon seeing our success, appeared to come out of his trance. At least he was making an attempt to come out of it.

"My people tell me that the VC are in the CORDS building (Civil Operations and Revolutionary Development), the Police Headquarters, the theater and the hotel," he said.

"Makes sense to me," I said.

The CORDS building was the Senior Provincial Advisor's headquarters. It was in a large compound and was in a strategic location in the downtown center.

The Police Headquarters definitely would be a target since it was near the CORDS building and it also had significant political importance and maybe the VC thought some of their own were held there.

The theater was located across the main square from the other two buildings and was probably the most solid structure of them all.

The My Loc Hotel was the tallest building in the city. It was at least five stories and was more than likely being used by the VC as an observation point to direct their movements within the city and as a forward observer position to direct mortar fire. A person could easily see the entire downtown area from that position as well as all the approaches to the city. It certainly was being used to follow our activities, I thought. We needed to clear the hotel but it was on the west side of town and we'd have to fight our way through the main enemy ground-forces located in the center of the city to get there. Then, if we made it, we'd be cut off. No, I thought, we need to take these positions as we get to them. First we needed to get these non-combatants out of danger.

"Where's The SEAL leader?" I asked Major Phoung, referring to Marcinko.

"I think he is over there," as he pointed to the radio room. Hoss and Gordy were right there, so I began briefing them on my immediate plans.

"Marcinko is trying to arrange for air support from Seawolves," Gordy interrupted.

"That's OK. We need to get moving. It'll be dark before they can get here and probably won't make it here until tomorrow, if they can come at all," I continued.

"We are going to head out for the Embassy House in just a few minutes and get the civilians back. Then we'll come right back and pick up you guys and head in to town. I'd like to find out more about the enemy situation before dark."

"We'll be ready, Drew," Gordy responded.

"I'll try to find some of my PRUs. They can be a big help."

"Yeah," Hoss said. "We could use all the help we can get."

Major Phoung interrupted by saying that the VC were also at his house and it looked like they were using it as a major headquarters. His voice cracked as he mentioned this, still thinking of his family.

"Yes," I said, "that would be a good place for them to operate from."

I told him that we saw several at Maggie's house and they had crawled through the back wall. He said that her house was directly across the alley from his house. That makes sense, I thought, not having made the connection before.

As I turned to resume talking with the SEALs, I detected the pride that our rescue party, including me, had. The SEALs were making small talk with the non-combatants.

Just then Marcinko walked up: "The platoon is ready to go if you need them."

"Sure, Dick, we're going into the city as soon as we get back from the Embassy House. We shouldn't be long. I'll just take Harry and Frank on this trip to the house. It will lighten our load some and we haven't had much action at the hospital lately. The Navy seems to have that place under control."

I started my Jeep and told the group of civilians to divide themselves into two elements and load up. Not wasting much time they quickly piled in without any further prodding. They were ready to go now. Obviously the civilians, who earlier thought they were out of danger, saw from the situation at the TOC that the crisis was far from over.

As we approached the downed trees my passengers became extremely quiet. I increased my speed and James, the agriculture advisor, looked at me like I was crazy. He placed both arms at his side and as we hit the tree he raised up as if to lighten the load.

Harry, still hanging on to the gun, reached over and steadied one of the civilians who lost his grip. We were getting our share of luck this day, I thought. We've passed by here four times now and haven't lost a man.

Jim and Westy met us as the two vehicles pulled into the crowded courtyard.

"Drew, what's your plan now?" Jim asked.

"I'd like to keep up the momentum. I plan to go back to the TOC and pick up the SEALs and head into town. We've got a lot to do before dark."

" Drew. Keep me informed how you're doing."

"I will, Jim, you can count on it but I'd still like to find out what's going on before dark. We need to find out where the enemy forces are concentrated. If they push their attack, we'll have a better idea where it's coming from. That could be helpful if we can get some air support."

"Good plan, Drew, but don't expect any air soon. I haven't been able to get much traffic through to either Can Tho or Saigon."

"Yeah, Jim, I'm not counting on the air."

"Have you talked with Marcinko?"

"Yeah, he volunteered his platoon to go with me."

"Great! They will be big help."

"They already have been," I answered back, "and the PBRs have given us the freedom to move back and forth by the hospital. I'm not sure if we would have been able to get this far without them.

"Let's go, Harry and Frank. Nago, you stay with Mr. Moore and help the Nungs defend the Embassy House tonight."

Nago was visibly disappointed but knew I was right.

"Jim," I asked, "could you send someone to the PRU compound and see what the situation is there? I'd like to get some of the PRUs to help in town. Tell Bao that I could use 15 or 20 men. Send them to town or to the TOC. We'll find them when they get in the area."

"OK, Drew I'll see what I can do. The Cambodes that were with you last night went on to the camp. Bao should know your situation from them."

"Yeah he's probably working on getting to us anyway."

"Drew, take care and we'll see you."

"Roger, I'll have the radio on our frequency."

Saying nothing more, we parted. I could tell that Jim wanted to go; but he knew that his place was at the Embassy House. Like a good leader, he was aware that at a time like this we all had jobs to do. Mine was to go after the Viet Cong; his was to coordinate our meager assets and defend the Embassy House. Only that way would we have a chance of coming out of this in one piece.

# CHAPTER 6

## TRAGEDY ON THE ROOF

The Jeep really felt frisky with a more-normal load as we easily hopped over the trees. It was getting a little quiet at the hospital, I thought, just as a shot popped overhead. Harry's smile disappeared as he let off a couple of rounds in response.

We pulled in to the TOC as our "automatic" gates swung open once again. The SEALs didn't waste any time. They had already divided into two groups and were ready to roll. Marcinko said that he'd stay at the TOC and be there if we got into trouble. He said he'd have the radio on our frequency, as he looked over and made note of the frequency dialed in on my PRC-25, still sitting between the front seats of my Jeep.

"Whatever you say," I said. "Let's go guys."

I heard numerous shouts of "Let's go getum" and "Let's kick some ass" as they piled into the two Jeeps. This time Risher claimed the .50. All nine of us were ready to do battle. No doubt the adrenaline was flowing. At this point we were all feeding on the excitement. We seemed to fuel each other and that is just what we needed if we were going to survive. We were clearly out-numbered. I wondered if the others had considered the odds.

It was getting late in the morning and as we approached the market square, it seemed like it was going to be a quiet drive through the streets. Suddenly a hail of small-arms fire interrupted the quiet. Now we were clearly committed.

"There is no going back now," I yelled.

Ted Risher made a comment about the vacation being over. Risher began to fire the .50 and soon after he got off the second burst, he yelled, "Aw, shit, the gun's jammed."

He cleared the breech. It fired only one round and stopped. He pulled back the handle and stripped off another round and fired. "Shit," he yelled.

"The gun's out of time," I yelled. "We can't do anything about it now."

I drove on. The loss of the .50 was not going to help. It had been a lifesaver all morning. The fire wasn't letting up and it seemed to be more disciplined. That didn't make me feel real good either. We were easy targets and I had thought the only reason we hadn't had any friendly casualties was the enemy's lack of fire discipline.

It's strange what goes on in a person's mind when the situation gets bad like it was then. Earlier I thought how easy it would be if the situation was reversed. I knew that a few well-placed and disciplined snipers would make short work of us. There were thousands of nooks and crannies to hide in: aim, hold your breath and squeeze! Now it appeared that they were under better control. The enemy small-arms fire wasn't going to let up.

We were further into town than any of us had been since the attack started. Out of the corner of my eye I could see black pajama-clad figures moving on the rooftops, running as if trying to keep up with us.

I turned to give instructions to the gunner since it appeared the .50 was working again. I could see that he had already focused on targets of his own.

I was approaching an intersection and was hoping that the VC running along the roofline to our right would be cut off by the cross street. They were, but I could see that there were more along the rooftops further ahead.

I pulled the Jeep up on the sidewalk and attempted to hug the buildings. This, I hoped, would block the VC's view of us from at least one side. On our side of the street ran an open drain that was about two feet wide and 18 inches deep. A couple inches of foul-smelling liquid ran in it. Every so often this drain was covered so vehicles could cross over, like we did, to gain access to some of the shops located in these buildings.

The SEALs quickly dismounted and dispersed into two elements to cover both sides of the streets. Two men remained on the .50, engaging the enemy along the rooftops with steady three-round bursts.

The two ground elements fired and maneuvered along the street. Without instructions, the element on one side of the street would fire to cover the other element as it advanced forward. I was moving with the group on the right, keeping my eye on the rooftops and the upper windows. My biggest concern was that we would bypass VC located in the buildings. We damn sure didn't want any to get between us and the .50-caliber. As long as the .50 was working, the enemy seemed to respect it and their firing almost stopped.

Just then two forms darted out and back into a doorway just behind Frank. At first I thought they were VC but their uniforms looked familiar. They had on the traditional leopard spots that my troops wore. I yelled to Frank that there were two PRUs behind him.

He stopped and turned to look back and I ran to make sure they were who I thought they were. Frank beat me there and was trying to talk with them. One appeared to have been wounded. He was crouched in the doorway, his carbine across his lap staring out in to the street with that proverbial 2,000-meter stare we see a lot of in this business.

Frank said, "Look at this, Drew! You aren't going to believe this shit."

Frank kind of chuckled as he held the guy's hair back and was pointing at his scalp. I couldn't believe it either. Just in front of his left ear at his hairline were two lumps about an inch long. They looked exactly like what they were—two AK-47 rounds tucked neatly under the skin between his skull and the skin. Both rounds obviously had entered over his left eye. The amazing thing was that there didn't appear to be much trauma to the wound. This was one of the luckiest guys I'd ever seen. He was going to be fine once he got over one hell of a headache.

It seemed that these two guys had been in the town celebrating Tet when the attack started. They had seen us earlier and were trying to link up with us. I told them to stay there until we pushed ahead. They would be able to provide cover for the .50 as we moved forward to get a better look.

Just as I was beginning to feel good about our situation, the .50 was firing single shots again. The enemy, seeing this, concentrated their fire toward the two men on the .50.

The SEALs and I engaged the enemy on the roofs. One sniper was a particular pain in the ass. He was dodging back and forth between two windows on the second floor of a building in the next block. I could see from my position the stubby end of a B-40 slowly emerge from the window.

I yelled this to alert the platoon and as I did, Risher engaged him with single-shot fire. It took a giant set of balls to stand up there and work that action knowing that the enemy knew he was firing single shot. Just as the gunner ducked back, I saw a .50 cal round hit the corner of the window where the sniper should have been. It was all over for him.

With this break, we climbed back on the two Jeeps and headed back to try the adjacent street. Again we ran into heavy resistance. I decided that we needed some heavier fire-power before we would be effective. The platoon agreed. I said that I had a 57mm-recoilless rifle back at the Embassy House. We had to have that if we were going to get anywhere.

We loaded up and covered the eight blocks to the TOC in just a few minutes. Not stopping at the TOC, we proceeded toward the Embassy House. It was a relief to see two familiar heads bobbing around inside the bunker as we approached the compound. I pulled in as far as I could to give the second vehicle room. Nago ran up to me and looked me over. We looked pretty ragged but, except for the wounded PRU, we hadn't sustained any serious injuries.

"Good job," Nago said, as he thoroughly checked me over.

"Nago, I want the 57. Go get it and 25 rounds of ammo. Take them out," as I animated this gesture. Nago didn't do bad with English but it made it easier when I could make gestures that he could understand.

"Give me 50 percent HE (high-explosive) and 50 percent anti-personnel," I called as he hurried off.

He knew what 50 percent was as we often used that term when we had a few drinks and Nago would make an imaginary line with his finger to mark off a percentage of the glass of beer or whatever was available for me to drink as a challenge. One has to know the importance of alcohol to the Oriental to appreciate this. It definitely was a macho trip for them, but one that worked.

"OK, sir," as he relayed this to the Nungs. Soon Vinh and two others returned with armloads of 57mm canisters. They quickly began tearing open the cardboard tubes, exposing the lethal little cylinders and stacked them neatly in the cargo area of Westy's Jeep. When they finished, Nago carefully laid the recoilless rifle on top of the load.

Seeing Jim, I told him of our plans and the need for the 57mm-recoilless rifle. He said that Bao was going to send some guys to help. They should be in town soon, he said.

"Great, we sure can use them. The whole time we were in the town we didn't see any friendlies (referring to GVN soldiers). I know there were some there but they didn't show themselves. They've probably been holed up since the attack started."

"Yeah, Drew, you can't count on any help from them."

"I'm not, Jim. We've got to go."

Once again, Jim had to see us off without him. Lin and Siew showed up with several loaves of French bread stuffed with more scrambled duck eggs. We were choking them down as I backed out of the compound. This time we stopped by the TOC to coordinate with Marcinko. I felt he needed to know what I had planned for his platoon.

"Where is the American?" I asked a Vietnamese sergeant. He pointed to the main bunker where I saw Marcinko standing at the entrance.

"Dick, we have a 57-recoilless rifle that we're going to take with us back to town. We need something to knock the hell out of the snipers from the roof. The .50 works great on the street but we need to get above the snipers to put them down for good. Whenever we fire on them with the .50, they duck out of the way and then move back in when we quit. The 57 should take out the position completely."

Marcinko seemed to like the idea.

"Where is Major Phoung?" I asked. He pointed to the radios and I moved away leaving Marcinko to talk with his men. I needed to get a better idea on how many more friendlies were in town. I didn't want to run into any with the SEALs. We had enough problems with the enemy—I didn't need to have our group fired on by friendlies.

"Major Phoung," I said as I walked up to him, "do you have any soldiers in the city?

"No. We have no troops in town. Only the ones who were on leave when the VC come."

"OK, we're going into the city again. If we see any of your soldiers, I'll send them here."

He thanked me. I was being sarcastic and he didn't even get it.

"Who's going with me?" I asked Marcinko.

He turned and I couldn't quite make it out but it sounded like he was asking for volunteers. Not saying a word, all reclaimed their places aboard the Jeeps. It crossed my mind that this seemed a bit strange. I've never been around a democratic combat unit before but I was glad for the company.

"Let's get going," I said, and we moved out one more time. Frank was in the suicide seat. Harry was again behind the .50. Ted and Doc were sitting on each side of the gun.

As we pulled out Harry bent down and helped Doc scoop arm-loads of spent .50-caliber casings out of the back, making room for their feet. This sight and the sound of the brass clattering on the street, as the Jeep accelerated, added to the excitement of the moment, causing the Vietnamese to look with astonishment as we headed back into certain action once again.

We were near the city center before we began to receive any significant enemy fire. Our next objective was the Police

Headquarters. When we got within two blocks of it we began to receive heavy small-arms fire. Rocket rounds could be heard to our front. So far I couldn't tell if we were their targets.

I pulled back on to the sidewalk and hugged the building. "Watch the roof above us," I yelled to the group. We were taking a small amount of fire from the police building.

"I need to make a quick recon of the objective. Cover me and get the 57 ready," I said, running toward the walled compound of the Police Special Branch Headquarters.

I crouched down and ran directly for the corner of the compound. It looked like that would give me cover from the front of the building where most of the fire was coming from. Upon approaching the wall, I received a short burst of fire from one automatic weapon and then it abruptly dropped off.

Glancing around the corner of the wall to get a better look, I saw what appeared to be friendlies peering over the wall toward me. At first I recognized the uniforms as those worn by the police and then I saw M-2 carbines in their hands. I still couldn't be sure that they weren't turncoats and were helping the VC from the inside.

One of them spoke English and called to me. I ran toward the main entrance and immediately was let in. The Vietnamese lieutenant grabbed my right hand with both of his as he vigorously shook it.

"Good to see you, sir," he said in very broken English. I recognized him from an earlier time when I transported a prisoner to the PIC.

"Where are the VC?" I asked.

"VC all over," he said as he made a 360-degree gesture with one arm, not letting go of my hand with the other.

Apparently some of his men were holed up together after spending the previous evening celebrating Tet. The policemen were in a building near where we were earlier this morning. They saw us and, seeing our successes, got their shit together and decided they could do it too. I congratulated them and said we were going to the CORDS compound.

"Where are the VC?" I asked again.

"Many VC at the CORDS and the movie (meaning the theater)."

"OK, I go now. No shoot Americans," I said smiling.

I left immediately and headed back to our force after being gone no more than four or five minutes. I thought it was a good thing that we hadn't fired on them with the 57-recoilless.

I crossed the street to where the SEAL platoon was waiting and immediately briefed them on the situation.

"The friendlies have that building and that part of the compound," pointing to where we could see the friendlies. "The VC still hold part of it. They said there were about two companies of VC and they were all around but mainly at the CORDS compound. It's too open here. We probably couldn't make it across without taking serious fire from over there," referring to the very wide street in front of the theater.

The wide intersection in front of the theater was near the actual center of the downtown area and the center of the VC-held area. Several streets entered this intersection, including the main entrance to the city from the west, giving it the appearance of a traffic circle.

I said we needed to go to the next street over and get on top of a building that would give us a good field of fire onto the CORDS building. We should be able to see that intersection from there too, pointing to the theater on the other side of the intersection. The CORDS building to our right, just behind the police building, was our main concern now.

I grabbed my radio and called the Embassy House to up-date our situation.

"Ringo, this is Westhaven, over."

"Roger, Westhaven."

"The friendlies have taken part of the Police Special Branch Headquarters. There aren't many friendlies there but they managed to kick the VC out. I'm not sure if they can hold on if they get hit again.'

"Roger, Westhaven, Bao sent some men to you. They are in their Ford pick-up. I think there are about 15 of them."

"Roger, Ringo, we can sure use them. Now we are going to try to take the CORDS building."

"Roger, Westhaven, We'll be here," was Jim's only reply.

We made a hasty U-turn in the middle of the street and headed back to the first intersection that would take us to the next street over. As we neared the intersection we received a lot of automatic-weapons fire. The rounds popped all around and cracked as they passed over-head.

I spotted a building that would give us an unobstructed view of the CORDS compound. It was at least a half story above the CORDS building. I slid the vehicle to a stop and the other Jeep slid right up to me, barely hitting the rear of mine.

"Gordy, send some men up on the roof. I'll stay down here and wait to send the 57 up on this rope. You guys cover them," pointing to the rest of the platoon. Gordy grabbed three of his men and took off. I tossed the rope to Ted as they went by.

Getting onto the roof wasn't going to be an easy task. The approach was in a narrow alley. There were a couple of fire escapes that led to a small rickety porch about half way up. From there, I wasn't sure how they were going to make it but I knew if anyone could, these guys could.

"I'll meet you on the roof after the recoilless is on its way up," I yelled to Gordy.

I watched as the four of them hustled off. I pressed myself to the building as three rounds struck the stucco next to my position. Peering around the corner into the alley to get a quick peek, I saw the SEALs disappear at a dead run. Still not sure how they were going to accomplish their task, I knew they would. In a short time they could be heard scurrying around halfway up the side of the building and a few hushed profanities accompanied their efforts as they climbed.

I risked another peek to check. As soon as I looked around the corner, I immediately was met with the expected rounds hitting next to my left side. Risking another look out of the corner of my eye I could see that they had already made it to the top of the roof, not taking more than a couple of minutes.

I hustled back to the front of the building. The firing had reached a steady level and everyone seemed to be busy at the time. I could hear Jack Saunders and Hoss tell each other how lucky they were. AK-47 rounds had struck the cement wall just between both of them and between their legs. They were in a discussion about "family jewels" or something to that effect.

Just then the rope was tossed over. Wasting no time, I quickly tied the recoilless rifle to it and yelled for them to pull it up. As the rope tightened and the recoilless began to ascend, I immediately turned to the alley to get up there myself.

I ran to the first fire escape that was still down and climbed up, taking three steps at a time to the rickety porch. Barely able to reach the edge of the porch roof, I managed to pull myself up and stopped to take a quick breath. One of the SEALs ran over and looked down from the rooftop.

"Drew, we've got a problem. Risher's been hit."

"How bad is it?"

"It's bad, we've got to get him back."

"Roger, I'll call the Embassy House and get a medivac started."

Hearing that, he disappeared back over the roofline.

Not being able to reach the Embassy House from the side of the building, I decided that I needed to get to the top for better reception. I climbed the last eight feet up the side of the building using the window ledges.

Again one of the SEALs called down from the roof for Doc to come up.

"Doc," he yelled, "Ted's been hit bad. Get up here quick."

Doc immediately rushed from his position along the side of the street and headed for the roof to join us. Seeing that it would take a while to get up that way, he turned back to the road where the SEALs were tearing a door off its hinges to get inside. He went to join them. It didn't take very long for them to get in.

"Ringo, this is Westhaven, over."

"Roger, Westhaven."

"We've got a problem. One of the SEALs has been hit bad. Relay to his boss the situation and request a medivac, over."

"Roger, Westhaven. What is your ETA (estimated time of arrival)?" Jim asked.

"We've got to get him down from a roof. Then we'll be there. I can't give you an ETA."

"Roger, Westhaven. I'll let you know what is going on when I find out something. Roger, out."

Following the radio call, I quickly ran over to the edge of the building where Gordy was holding Ted's head in his lap and talking to Ted, trying to get a response. There was none, only the frustrated look of someone trying to get words out but couldn't. Ted had taken a hit over the left eye by a single round, probably from an AK-47 that had been giving us hell since we arrived at that building. Our luck had run out.

Ted didn't look good. A two-inch string of gray matter had already leaked from the long furrow that ran across the top of his head. "They're working on the medivac," I said.

No one really expected the medivac to make a difference but it's what you do in that situation.

"Let's get him off of here," Gordy yelled to the others. "Doc's on his way up."

Jack on one end and Gordy on the other grabbed Ted and quickly carried him to where they had set the same door they had torn off its hinges and had carried to the roof. I picked up his weapon and covered them as they proceeded down the stairs they had come up. The VC sniper fire hadn't let up and I knew the litter party would catch hell when they hit the street. From the amount of fire, it was hard to imagine that Ted was the only one hit.

I don't know how they did it, but in no time the two of them carrying Ted were downstairs onto the street. Doc had already started an IV and was following alongside the makeshift litter. Somewhere along the way, he had applied a dressing over the wound. Doc and Gordy were trying to get a response from Ted but none came.

I provided cover for them from the top of the building as they concentrated on Ted. As soon as they left the roof, I ran to the side of the building. Our situation could get real bad very quickly. The enemy knew we had a problem and would try to take advantage of the situation. I had to keep an eye on how this drama was unfolding.

I retraced my steps and hopped down off the porch. When I hit the street I grabbed my handset from the radio and called the Embassy House to check on the progress of the medivac. While on the radio, I saw a familiar sight. It was the PRU truck moving slowly down the street toward our position. I couldn't see Bao, but recognized some of the others. There were about 15 of Bao's best men and one had our M-60 machine gun.

Bao was good, I thought, to send this team. They were a feisty bunch. I yelled to them. They immediately recognized me, and several of the PRUs jumped out of the back of the vehicle and joined the rest of the SEALs in securing the street.

Tran, Bao's deputy, came up to me and surprised me by saying my name since I've never heard him say anything in English before.

"Mister Trew," he uttered, "Beaucoup VC" and smiled.

"Yes, beaucoup VC," and I pointed toward the CORDS building and the theater.

He shook his head understanding and barked orders to his men. I motioned them to stay there for a minute. I said "one man" and pointed to my forehead making a sound like a shot. He understood and called his medic from the truck. "It's OK, caw bauxie," I told him, indicating we had a doctor.

The truck came under heavy fire and quickly pulled into the alley for cover. The PRUs fanned out and began firing in all directions as did the SEALs on the street. I ducked back in to the alley and ran to where Gordy, Schwalenberg and Doc were moving toward us.

Tran, seeing the three men struggling with Ted, ordered two of his men to help. Doc, expressing great concern for Ted, shouted, "We need a medivac soon!"

"Doc," I said, "we aren't going to get a medivac into the city under these conditions and I doubt if there's one within 50 miles of this place.

Doc said, "I know, but we've got to try."

I told him, "I've already called it in, Marcinko knows about the situation and I'm sure he's on it."

Doc knew it was probably hopeless but that didn't make the situation any easier. He felt responsible for the platoon and knew he had to try.

"The PRUs are here." I said. "They just drove up. We can take Ted back in the truck. Doc and Ted will go in the back of the truck along with two others. The rest of us will go in the Jeeps."

I conveyed this to Tran. He quickly grasped the situation and barked orders to his men who responded immediately. Firing as they pulled back from their positions, they were back in the truck in seconds, making room for Ted and Doc.

Not wasting any more time, I floored my Jeep and headed back toward the TOC yelling "di di mau," the Vietnamese words for let's go. The big Ford pick-up made a U-turn and pulled in right after me. As it did, it received several rounds of small-arms fire that struck the hood. I could hear the familiar sound of the M-60 as it responded. The other Jeep closed in to cover from the rear.

As we proceeded through the now familiar streets, I felt glad to have the extra firepower of my PRUs. Even though we had our first casualty, I felt we had been fairly lucky. We were able to move about the city and were able to rescue nine non-combatants.

No doubt, I was trying to justify the loss of Ted with our successes. I also felt the loss the SEALs had for their buddy. Ted had done a fine job and never hesitated when I told him to get on that roof. Now wasn't the time to think about this. We still had a job to do and we were a long way from getting it done.

The gates of the TOC once again swung open. Our welcoming committee was not so jubilant as in the past, no doubt already having heard of our casualty. Marcinko ran up and looked into each Jeep for Ted, shouting, "How bad is it! How bad is it!"

One of the SEALs pointed to the pick-up, not saying a word. Marcinko stopped in his tracks as he saw Risher's lifeless body laying in the back of the truck.

"What happened?" he asked.

"It doesn't matter right now how it happened, You need to get him to an LZ (landing zone) and out of here," Harry responded.

Marcinko grabbed half of his platoon and said, "We need to use your Jeep to take Ted to the LZ at the south end of town by the airfield."

"Sure," I told him. "Take both Jeeps and the truck too. You may need them."

Doc made a couple improvements on Ted's battle dressings and said they were as ready as they can be. Marcinko climbed into my Jeep and sped toward the edge of town.

After they left the compound. I thought I'd better call the Embassy House and let Jim know what the situation was.

"Ringo, this is Westhaven, over."

Jim answered almost instantly. No doubt he was standing by the radio, as he said he would.

"Ringo, three vehicles are heading your way with our casualty. They may drive right by you or they may stop to get on the boats. I'm not sure their exact plans. I think they have an ETA of a medi-vac."

"Roger," Jim said. "The Navy has the medivac request so it should be in the works. I'm not sure how long it will take to get here. I don't think they have left Can Tho yet. The enemy is still putting pressure on Can Tho so they still have their hands full down there."

"Roger, Ringo, I'm going to take the remaining SEALs with me back into town as soon as the pick-up gets back. I linked up with my guys (referring to the PRUs and not wanting to convey that fact in the clear for the enemy to intercept)."

"Roger. I understand you have linked up."

This was a good time to take a quick break. I joined my group of PRUs, who didn't go with the SEALs, in one corner of the compound under a large shade tree. The PRUs were respected—or rather, feared—by the Vietnamese regular military. For this reason, they never really associated much with each other. So the PRUs found a quiet place away from the excitement. The GVN soldiers left them very much alone. This fear or respect probably is attributable more to the power we had than any other single factor.

A young Vietnamese soldier approached carrying a large glass of water, saying "nuuoc lan," meaning cold water, and gestured for me to drink. I gratefully accepted the offer but thinking that a cold beer would really be nice. I gulped the water down and I doubt if a cold beer could have tasted any better.

I commented on how this was good like Ba Muoi Ba, a Vietnamese beer called "thirty-three", reportedly made with formaldehyde. My troops laughed at this and made similar gestures about all the other good things in life.

I often sparked conversation with my troops in this manner as a way to overcome the language barrier and to establish rapport. The basic language of soldier between soldier is universal and usually can be understood, and we were no different.

Another young Vietnamese brought to me and the PRUs a plate of rice and a couple of very small fish placed on top. They also brought a small cup of the ever-present nuuoc mam, fermented fish sauce, which really did a great job of stinking up the rice. The thought to share was pretty damn generous, despite the meager portions, since supplies probably were getting very scarce right now. I was sure that no one had left the TOC compound, except for us, since the attack began about 12 hours before.

Gordy Boyce and the SEALs were in a separate group relaxing and no doubt going over the recent events. The grave situation concerning one of their own was on everyone's mind. I could hear them on the radio with the others. Soon after they finished, Gordy came over and said that he had just talked with Marcinko.

I asked, "How is the medivac going?"

"They are securing an LZ for the Helo and some of the platoon are with Risher on the boats," Gordy replied. "We're supposed to stay here at the TOC until he gets back. I know you want to go back into town soon but we need to stay until Marcinko gets back."

"How long will it be before they make it back?"

With an extremely remorseful look on his face, Gordy answered, "Drew, I don't know when but, how can I say it?"

"Go on, what's the problem?"

"The real issue is that the Commander doesn't want to lose anymore SEALs to sniper fire. He says we are too valuable to lose like that."

I told him, "Hey, no problem, we appreciate the help you've given so far. I'm sorry about Ted but I can't do anything about that. I've got to go. Have them send the pick-up truck back. I need it ASAP to go back to town."

"Will do, Drew."

Rex Johnson, who I had gotten to know fairly well, came up to me and said, "Take care of yourself." A very concerned look was on his face as he added. "We'll be here if you call for help."

"Thanks, buddy," as I slapped him on the shoulder. "Hey, I know you would go if you could. Don't worry about it, OK."

"Drew, I mean it. Call if you get into a jam. We'll come no matter what."

"I know you will," I told him as I turned and walked toward my troops and waited for the truck.

In less than 20 minutes the PRUs who had escorted Ted and Doc and some of the SEALs roared into the compound. I let the PRUs finish their brief reunion as they no doubt explained to the others the ordeal of going by the hospital.

I could make out that they had stopped and attempted to move some of the deadfall. Before they had cleared it all, the VC had started to snipe at them. They all joked at each other as they explained the antics of how each had rushed back to the vehicle as it started to go without them.

Combat is amazing. When there are no casualties it can actually be humorous. Much like it was when we first started. We were doing the same. Now that we had a serious casualty, it hit close to home. Our group was a little quiet now that the table has turned. The SEALs will get their chance again!

It has to be said that the decision for the SEALs not to go back into the city at that time was a command decision and not a group one. There is no doubt in my mind everyone would have gone back in if they hadn't received orders not to.

# CHAPTER 7

## KEEPING UP
## THE MOMENTUM

I was making a last minute check of my gear and as I picked up my PRC-25 it broke the silence.

"Westhaven, this is Ringo, over."

"Go ahead, Ringo."

"Roger, Westhaven, I just got word from the PSA (Provincial Senior Advisor) that there were two Filipinos at the CORDS compound last night. Check on them when you get there."

"OK," I responded. "How are the civilians and Maggie?"

"They are fine now. We just put them on the PBRs and they are on their way down river."

"Great! We're going back into the city in a couple of minutes."

"Who's going with you?" Jim asked.

"The men who Bao sent are going. We'll be in their truck. So put the word out that the green pick-up are good guys."

"Roger, Westhaven. Are the other U.S. going?"

Still not wanting to refer to the SEALs in the clear over the radio. I replied, "Negative. They are waiting for their leader per his instructions."

"Roger, Westhaven. I wish they were going with you."

"Yeah but we'll be OK. Westhaven out."

With that, I called to the PRUs who were still in their little corner of the compound. "Let's di di and san cong," which roughly meant let's go kill VC. They all quickly gathered their gear and climbed aboard the green pick-up.

Three of us piled into the front seat and the rest of the PRUs climbed in the back. Not knowing the translation for the CORDs compound, I just pointed and shouted for the driver to go in the general direction of the downtown and he apparently understood.

He floored the vehicle, not waiting for the guard to open the gate. The gate barely opened in time and the men all yelled obscenities at the remaining Vietnamese. I was sure that had the gate not opened, we would have rammed through. There obviously was no love lost between the two groups, and my guys never missed a chance to rub it in. This time they were ridiculing them for not going out of the compound to fight the VC.

When we reached the first intersection we started to receive sniper fire. Continuing down the street, just before making the next turn, a squad of black pajama-clad men with weapons ran across the street about two blocks ahead. I yelled over to Tran, "Phuc kich, phuc kich, VC phuc kich!" The driver didn't let up as he closed in on them. It must have finally registered to Tran that I was probably right. The VC were going to ambush us on the street. He yelled at our driver to pull over and stop. The truck bumped over the drain system and hugged the building so close that the three of us had to exit on the street side.

The enemy, on seeing that we weren't going to move into the killing zone, initiated their ambush with a B-40 rocket. The rocket slammed into the building on the opposite side of the street. As debris and smoke engulfed our position, I knew we must have casualties. One man yelled that he was hit. Tran ran to him and seeing that he was only slightly injured, pulled him by the collar and threw him on to the curb yelling instructions for everyone to kill the enemy.

The enemy began maneuvering down both sides of the street toward us. The rounds were hitting all around our positions. Tran saw the RPG (rocket propelled grenade) position the same time I did and yelled, "Be bon muoi" (meaning B-40) as we directed our fire to the second-floor window about 100 meters down the street. The launcher fell to the street and we all shifted our fire to the others.

It appeared that we had at least a platoon-sized force to our front. We had to maneuver if we were going to get out of this one. I was glad to have this crew with me, I thought as the fire intensified. By this time rounds were hitting all around us. I could feel the sting of the shattered concrete hit my face and the back of my neck. What we needed now was luck. The VC were systematically advancing toward us. Each time they secured a piece of real estate, they left someone to secure it as others pushed forward.

I shouted to Tran and held up five fingers and pointed to my chest and made a sweeping gesture with my other arm. Acknowledging my intentions to circle around from the other street on the next block, he yelled and six men hurried to my side.

Not wanting to waste time trying to explain what we were going to do, I stood and ran back toward the intersection. The six PRUs dropped in behind me and we hugged the building as we ran to the adjacent street. My idea was that if we could get away undetected, we could surprise the VC from behind.

I was counting on their thinking that all they had opposing them were those to their front. If we could surprise them from the rear or from the rooftops, we could break up their momentum. It was a simple plan but I had no idea where the rest of the enemy units were.

The CORDS compound was behind the attacking force about one block away. I knew that this was a key stronghold and might give us a problem if they spotted us. The streets were wide where we were now and wouldn't give us much cover.

As we trotted along the sidewalk, parallel to the street Tran was on but one block over, one of my men made a light whistle sound to get my attention. We stopped abruptly and he pointed up on the roof just above us. As I peered out from the cover of the building, I saw a VC figure dashing back and forth looking frantically over the side of the building. One of the PRUs leaned out as if to pick him off. I put my finger to my lips and shook my head, whispering, "No shoot." I didn't want to give our position away for one enemy KIA (killed in action). He understood and we waited a couple seconds until he moved off. The fire from the other street hadn't slacked off and I knew their ammunition wouldn't hold out much longer. My main concern now was that if the VC tried the same tactic we were using, we would be in big trouble.

We pushed on and as we got close to the next street, I halted our group. Not making a sound, we took a quick breather. Just then one of my troops pointed to the sidewalk as a small stream of liquid appeared and slowly tracked toward the curb. It wasn't raining, so the only thing it could be was someone relieving himself in the alley. The small stream arched toward me close enough to touch, which I did, and after a quick examination, confirmed that it was urine.

We couldn't take the chance, so we readied ourselves for a dash across the alley. One PRU held a grenade for the count of three and tossed it into the alley as we all ran across. There was no evidence of a survivor, so we pushed on.

Time was the issue now. As we neared the last street before the CORDS compound, I was sure small-arms fire was coming from inside the compound. Hopefully there were other friendlies in there. We were going to need all the help we could get. I couldn't think about that now, but the idea of some allied assistance was a welcome thought.

We turned left and headed to flank the VC platoon that was engaging Tran and the boys. This put us on the opposite side of the street of the CORDS compound. I could hear several rocket rounds go off with a whoosh as they passed by and a second later the explosion.

I directed three men to move along our present course. The other three went with me and we ran at an angle across the street in order to have a better field of fire. Doing this, we could support the other three as they attacked toward the rear of the VC. The VC were concentrating so much on Tran and his men that they didn't see us approach from behind.

My element and the other three saw the VC at the same time. I didn't have to give the signal. All of us opened up at the same time, scarcely 30 meters from their rear. The enemy were fully exposed and suddenly found themselves surrounded. Tran and his men seeing this immediately assaulted the enemy.

We could see four or five on the rooftops starting to throw hand grenades down on Tran's element. We managed to drop two of them before they threw. Two more managed to toss their grenades but because of the heavy volume of fire from our position, the grenades exploded in the middle of the street. They did more to break up the ambush than inflict casualties on us.

Several enemy dashed back into the doorways from where they had just come, leaving eight dead behind in the street. In just a few seconds it became quiet. We checked each other out for injuries. We only had a couple minor ones that could wait to be treated. The PRUs no doubt were feeling good about their success and weren't going to stop our momentum for anything, especially for a couple shrapnel wounds.

We still had several hours of daylight. I pointed to my watch and said to Tran, "nam phut," meaning five minutes we go. Answering in Vietnamese, he understood and asked each of his men how much ammunition they had. Most of them were armed with the Swedish-K like the one I carried that used 9mm and the others had U.S.-made M-2 carbines that used .30-caliber ammunition.

Between us we had 600 rounds of 9mm ammo for the Swedish-Ks. That worked out to about two 38-round magazines apiece. Those armed with the M-2's had about 45 rounds apiece.

The PRUs began stripping the AK-47 ammo pouches off of the enemy dead and gathered up three workable weapons. We hadn't used many grenades so we had plenty.

The M-60 machine gun ammo was our biggest concern. It looked like we had less than 100 rounds for it. Not a whole hell of a lot to do battle with but everyone was hot to go so as not to lose our momentum. We pushed on.

Our plan was to backtrack the way the seven of us had done when we encircled the enemy a few minutes earlier. It looked like the best route at the moment since we hadn't received any fire from across the street after we opened up. I thought that if we could get to the Filipinos in an hour, we'd have another four or so to extricate ourselves and get back to the TOC or the Embassy House. I didn't want to have to drive by the TOC or even approach it after dark.

We had plenty of daylight to do what we needed if we didn't make a wrong move and get trapped. There wasn't anyone to help us if we did. Also we'd be fired on for sure by Major Phoung's trigger-happy defenders and spending the night in the city with this small force and low on ammo just didn't make sense.

The six PRUs and I trotted along the sidewalk while the rest rode at slow speed. If we hadn't feared losing the vehicle, we all would have gone on foot. That was by far the best tactical way to approach. We couldn't leave the truck unattended and leaving someone to guard it was dumb. So we moved out with it.

This time we were going to try to take the CORDS building and see if the Filipino technicians were still alive. As soon as we made the second turn and faced the CORDs compound about one block to our front we started receiving steady small-arms fire. Luckily they weren't trained snipers, because if they were, they would have been able to pick some of us off easily. Instead, they chose to engage us with conventional tactics, which was all right with me.

Tran indicated he would go around with his group like we had done earlier. Hopefully he would be just as successful because we wouldn't be able to hold out as long due to our ammo situation. OK, I said, and gave him the proverbial thumbs up.

He yelled for his men to climb in the truck and they immediately headed out. Not wanting to get bogged down, the rest of us covered each other as we leapfrogged down both sides of the street. I sensed that Tran had run into a problem as the fire from the next street over had increased. I could make out the steady rattle of the M-60.

Our hands were full as we continued our steady but really slow movement toward the CORDS compound. Suddenly two VC stepped out into the street. It looked as if we surprised them because they hesitated firing on us. They probably heard the truck leave and thought we had all gone. We fired at both of them, and one dropped in his tracks and the other limped off into the alley. Two PRUs went with me to pursue him. As soon as he reached the alley, he fired over his shoulder without aiming and the shots went wild. We followed him for a few meters and decided to let him go. Looking up at the tall buildings closing in over us in the alley was spooky. We were pretty vulnerable to anyone on the roof with hand grenades and he just wasn't worth getting sucked into an ambush. "Let's go," I said to the others and they quickly agreed. We turned to join the other four at the head of the alley.

For no real reason the enemy seemed to pull back. Possibly remembering what happened earlier, they moved off toward the direction of the encircling force. Whatever the reason, we were taking advantage of the situation and before we knew it, we were on the same side of the street as the compound.

I plastered myself against the outside wall and tried to catch my breath. I really felt conspicuous, silhouetted against that white wall. For some reason, the story of the ambush of the wood-cutting party of soldiers at Piney Creek during the Indian Wars came to mind. I hoped that history wouldn't repeat itself here. If it was going to, I thought, it was too late to save ourselves because we were definitely committed. Here we were, seven of us, low on ammo, couldn't communicate worth a damn and we were literally knocking on Victor Charles door. Knock! Knock!

I couldn't wait for Tran. He was giving us valuable time that we weren't going to waste. I motioned to my men that we needed to move. They understood since we were really exposed, pressed up against that wall. If we were attacked from either side or from where we had just come, we would be completely in the open. At present we were receiving sporadic small-arms fire. It was only a matter of time before the enemy would get their shit together and organize an assault against us.

The CORDS compound consisted of a very large, impressive two-story cement and block building and several smaller buildings of similar construction behind a wall that encircled the complex. The red-tiled roof of the main building was multi-leveled with many steep slopes. The wall directly in front of us was in front of the main building about 15 feet.

The space between the wall and the building looked as if had been covered by a roof that extended the entire length of the wall to make several rooms used for offices. This gave the appearance that the main building actually reached the wall. Only a few of the rooms in this addition had windows so we had some concealment from the defenders.

I could hear the shuffling of footsteps that were unmistakably made by men with heavy sandals like the ones the VC wore. The PRUs seemed to be getting a bit nervous, knowing the enemy was just a few steps away. By the scurrying around and the high-pitched exited voices, I knew that the VC were getting organized.

We had to move fast. I needed to get on the roof. This place was as good as any to start.

I motioned to my guys that I was going up on the roof and they were to watch for the VC. They looked at me like I was crazy. In fact one grabbed my arm and said. "No can do! Beaucoup VC."

I'm sure the wall was a bit intimidating to them as well because of its height. I had a good six to eight inches on the tallest of my PRUs. I pushed his arm away and grabbed the edge of the roof and started to wiggle my way up. I felt the PRUs pushing on my legs to help me up. Under their breath I could hear them saying this was crazy. I didn't care what they thought as long as they did their job and so far I didn't expect them to do anything but that.

The overhang on the roof was about two feet so I was glad they were there to give me a shove. A B-40 rocket hit the roof to my left. It was probably fired from a position close to where the theater was located.

I began to hear the high pitched "thunk" of light mortars and waited for the rounds to hit. When two rounds hit the street to our rear and two rounds hit the roof I was on, I knew that they had us bracketed. I scrambled up the slope of the roof, grabbing at the tiles that had been loosened by the rocket and mortars. AK-47 rounds began hitting around me as I climbed.

I pulled the Swedish-K around to my front in the ready position as I continued up to the top of the first level of the roof. If I could get to the top, I might be able to see inside the compound to the right of the main building. I reached the low wall that overlooked the court-yard. This short wall ran along the top of the roof I was on.

As I turned to glance back to see if the PRUs were following me, a B-40 slammed onto the roof and loosened the already shaky tiles. I started to slide and picked up momentum like an avalanche. I felt my feet give way through the roof. I grabbed anything I could to keep from going through. I fell through to my waist and the Swedish-K, which was hanging around my neck, slapped me in the face as it hung up on the rafters.

I had a good hold of the rafters and started to raise myself up. Small-arms fire started coming up, blasting the already loose tiles. I knew from the report of the weapons that the VC were just below me in one of the rooms.

I started to lose my grip and I felt myself sliding down. I momen-tarily was hung up in the rafters by the radio on my back. The rounds continued to erupt around me, further loosening the tiles. As I fell through, I worried about my Swedish-K getting fouled with loose mortar and tile since it fires from the open-bolt position, exposing the chamber. As I glanced into the chamber to see if it was clear, it smacked me once more in the face as it again hung up momentarily.

I fell the rest of the way through the rafters. As I dropped to the ground I could see two VC scarcely two meters from my feet. I don't know how they missed. They would have done better if they had grabbed my feet. Both had apparently emptied their magazines at the same time and seemed to fumble trying to reload. I fired my Swedish-K and both fell to the ground.

Relieved that my weapon wasn't jammed, I pulled a grenade off my belt and held it in my left hand with the pin pulled. Running through the doorway into the courtyard I saw two VC to my right, firing over their shoulders. They disappeared behind the corner of a small building within the courtyard. I ran at a crouch and tossed the grenade around the corner as I hugged the wall. After the explosion, I rushed from my position and saw one VC dead on the ground and could hear one moaning.

Running toward the sound as the dust and smoke cleared from the explosion, I saw a form, still on the ground, moving to pick up his weapon. Not wanting to give my position away, I kicked him in the head.

Reaching a small corner, I dropped to one knee and took a couple breaths. The PRUs were up on the roof I had just come through. They were scrambling up the tiles and yelling to me. I wish they weren't doing that. I wasn't alone and the last thing I needed was for the VC in there with me to find out that I was in there by myself.

I also wondered if Tran had made it in the truck. Just then, the radio broke the silence.

"Westhaven, Ringo, over." It sounded as if a speaker was on full blast but I knew better. Even though the volume was on low, I felt conspicuous in the open talking on the radio with the enemy a few feet away.

I whispered a response. "Wait, Ringo, I'm busy. Out."

I couldn't afford the time to take the radio off of my back and turn it off. Just then, to my left front, I saw three or four enemy soldiers. This time they were wearing green fatigues indicating that there were at least two different main-force units involved in this attack. The others we had fought earlier were wearing black pajamas.

I thought, please don't call me back Jim.

The PRUs were calling, "Mr. Trew! Mr. Trew." Shit, I said under my breath, that's all I need, they're going to get me blown away.

Two B-40's hit the roof where their voices were coming from. There was a silence and then the sound of tiles slipping and clanking as the PRUs moved up the roof again. I was relieved that they were OK but also glad that the VC gunners got their attention and they quit calling to me.

I looked up and could see one of them peering over the low wall that followed the roofline they were on. He was trying to look down in the courtyard but not wanting to expose himself any more than he had to. Almost as soon as he showed himself two rounds hit the base of the wall just below his head. He quickly disappeared. I could make out his two elbows raised up, making a motion like he was pulling a pin from a grenade! Aw shit, I thought, he's going to toss a grenade down on to me. No wonder he was calling me. He wanted to make sure I was not in the way.

One thing for certain is that the Vietnamese love hand grenades and my troops were no different in that regard. If they had a dozen with them, they would use them all before they joined me down here.

"OK! OK!" I yelled, once again using this popular American phrase to communicate. It worked because I heard them shouting to one another that "Mr. Trew" was there.

This gamble had mixed returns. It kept my own guys from blowing me away but it gave away my position. Almost immediately I received fire from several different directions, all within 20 to 30 feet. Some good jungle cover would be nice now and a little darkness wouldn't hurt either, I thought as I returned fire.

I ran to take cover in a room off to my left from where I had come earlier. Firing only a short burst because of being critically low on ammo, I made it to the room I had fallen into earlier. Often in a tight situation like this, I changed magazines before they were empty so that a full one was always available. This time I was counting the rounds as they were used. Seven, eight, nine. About twenty-seven left in this magazine.

I glanced out of my hiding place to see if the PRUs had made it down into the courtyard. No, they were still on the roof but they could see me. Two Viet Cong were firing from a position just below them. I pointed to the VC position and one of the PRUs acknowledged my gesture with a hand grenade held up in the air for me to see. I gave him a thumbs up and he immediately tossed the grenade down directly onto the two unsuspecting VC.

Using this diversion, I moved to a position closer to where I had last seen some VC firing on me.

As I made my way toward them, I saw someone duck into a small room which appeared to be an outside closet that protruded into the narrow passageway I was moving in. For no other reason than the guy was wearing unusual looking clothes for a VC, I yelled at the figure just as the door closed behind him. The door slowly opened again and I almost changed my mind. I could see a dirty, dark face peek out and a weapon in his hands. On his head was a red bandanna. I raised my weapon to my waist as if to fire. Before I did, I recognized him as one of the Filipino technicians who worked for Mr. Tull. He responded, not knowing that I had recognized him: "I'm Arturo Gatpayat."

"OK, Arturo, you can come out."

He yelled, "Tolibas, it's Mr. Drew! Come out!"

Across the passage way I could see a door slowly open as Dennis Tolibas cautiously emerged from his hiding spot, also looking a lot like a VC. They must have had a scary night, jockeying around from position to position just a few feet from the VC.

Both men appeared to be all right. Arturo had a slight eye wound.

Grenades were going off all around us and the sounds of spent bullets clattering against the cement became real evident.

"The PRUs are coming," I said to Dennis and Arturo as I herded them into "my" room. We crouched down just a few feet from the two dead VC that I had killed after falling through the roof. I wasn't sure if either Dennis or Arturo saw them.

"Let me see your eye," I said to Arturo. He let me look at it but said that it was all right.

"There is a young girl in there also," Arturo said as he called under his breath. I could see a pretty girl of about 18 slowly appear in the passageway from the small closet where Arturo had been hiding.

"Come," I yelled, and she trotted over to the doorway and ducked in to join us.

Not saying much, she grabbed my arm and began thanking me many times.

"OK, OK," I said. "We must go now. We aren't free yet. We must climb out of here."

Saying to Dennis and Arturo, "We need to get over this wall to the street and I hope the PRUs are there."

"We're ready Drew. Which way?"

"Follow me," I said, not knowing exactly how we were going to get over the wall. We certainly weren't going to go back the way I had come down and in.

We trotted out of that room and I could see my men looking into the courtyard. At first I believe they thought the VC had captured me, seeing the two Filipinos following me. They really did look like VC. I found out later that they had disguised themselves for just that reason. It almost got them killed, once by me and now by my troops.

I waived my weapon so my troops could see that I was still armed. Seeing this, they immediately started firing over our heads as we approached the wall. As if they had been put there for our convenience, boxes and furniture had been piled up against the wall by the VC so they could climb up there to fire on us as we approached earlier.

I hopped up part of the way and extended my arm for the young girl. I pulled her up as Arturo gave her a boost and easily lifted her light body up to the rooftop above my head. The PRUs pulled her through and passed her to the others on the street.

I grabbed each of the other two and pulled them up to my level, then boosted them up to the guys on the roof. During this time two PRUs were providing covering fire into the courtyard. I pulled myself over the short wall on top of the roof. As soon as I did, I could see the green Ford pick-up parked just below the building. Great, I thought, now we'd be able to get these three back soon.

I took this opportunity to give Jim and Westy a situation report. No doubt they would be anxious to hear from us.

"Ringo, this is Westhaven, over."

"Roger, Westhaven, go ahead," came an almost instant response.

"We are at the CORDS building and have the two Filipinos with us and one Vietnamese girl. They are a bit shook up but are OK."

"Roger, Westhaven, good news. I'll tell the PSA (Provincial Senior Advisor, meaning Mr. Flashpoler the acting PSA)."

"You may want to ask him if there is anything that he needs checked out before we leave."

"Roger, wait one."

In just a couple minutes Jim called back and said, "Westhaven, he'd like you to check on his safe. There are some important documents that shouldn't fall into enemy hands."

"Roger. I'll check on them."

"Westhaven, don't risk your ass just for the papers. Understand!"

"Roger, I'll just take a quick look and see if the safe is intact.

Westhaven out."

I shut off the radio and slid down to the edge of the roof to tell the PRUs that I would be going back into the compound. When I approached the edge of the building, I could see that my men still weren't certain of the status of the Filipinos. They had them against the wall and for a minute I thought they were going to shoot them. The Vietnamese girl was pleading their case, but for fear of retaliation, she wasn't pressing the issue too hard.

I jumped down from the roof and stood between the Filipinos and their executioners. "Tran! No VC," I yelled and put my arm around Arturo and Dennis indicating that we were friends. I could see that they must have thought I had captured them. They still looked a hell of a lot like VC.

I laughed and for a second everyone saw the humor of the situation. The last to join in were the two Filipinos and the young girl.

I told Dennis and Arturo that I was going back into the main building to check on the safe. They both looked at me like it was a crazy idea.

"Look guys, you just stay here. I'll only be a few minutes. Just stay with them," as I pointed to the PRUs. Still not sure of their safety, they seemed to hesitate at that suggestion.

"Go ahead, it's OK. I'll be right back." I handed the radio to them and said to keep an eye on it. Knowing that they worked as radiomen for Mr. Tull, I thought that they would take this as a mission and relax. It seemed to work and they went over to the truck and sat down behind it out of the line of sniper fire.

I was trying to explain to Tran that I needed to go back in to the compound to check on some papers. I wasn't having much luck, not only because of my limited vocabulary but because it seemed like a dumb idea. It actually sounded really dumb to me as I was trying to find the right words. It just didn't seem to come out right.

The author with some of the Nungs standing around the jeep with the fifty caliber machine-gun a few days prior to the TET offensive. Nago is on the left with his rifle at the ready. (Dix collection)

One of my PRU teams taken at the PRU camp soon after the TET offensive. (Dix collection)

One of the Nungs firing the fifty caliber from my jeep near Nha Bang, just west of Chau Phu city. (Dix collection)

Dennis Drady (with the radio) and Jack Saunders taken across the Bassac river from the Embassy House taken in May following TET. (Dix collection)

From left to right, Dennis Drady, Frank Scollise (center rear) and Joe Albrecht. Joe was not with us during the TET offensive. He was later killed on Nui CoTo while we were operating with another SEAL platoon commanded by Bob Gormly. (Dix collection)

From front to rear, Rex Johnson, the author and Harry Humphries taking a break just after making contact with a small enemy force while operating in the An Phu district just north of Chau Phu. (Dix collection)

Taken inside the Embassy House compound, shows the author with Frank Thornton and Jim Moore, aka, Jim Monroe. (Dix collection)

Bao, the one eating with one of the Nungs. (Dix collection)

Maggie's house soon after TET. The rescue jeeps were parked directly in front of her Scout. (Dix collection)

Maggie's International Scout in front of her house soon after the TET offensive. (Dix collection)

The two rescue jeeps. The authors in the front with the fifty mounted in the rear and Westy's parked behind. (Dix collection)

A rare occasion where Bao and the author relaxing together. (Dix collection)

The photo was taken during the initial construction of a new camp far to the north on the Bassac near the Cambodian border. Bao, in black pajamas, is shown supervising camp placement. (Dix collection)

One of two specially configured sixteen foot Boston Whalers that were used for travel on the river system and for our E&E plan. Note the M-60 machine-gun mounted on the bow. A small craft with twin sixty-five Mercury motors that could really move! (Dix collection)

The author looking across the river into Cambodia with Nago, as always, close behind. (Dix collection)

The jeep Sergeant Williams was in when he was killed trying to reinforce the city during the TET offensive. (Dix collection)

The bridge on the Tinh Binh road that was blown by the VC. The destruction isolated the city for several critical hours during the initial phase of the attack. (Dix collection)

The author coordinating operations the day following the recapture of the city. (Dix collection)

The road to the south of the city after it was mined by the VC, further cutting us off for awhile. The PRU pick-up truck is on one side and the author's jeep on the other. (Dix collection)

A typical building in Chau Phu during the TET offensive. (Dix collection)

One of the major buildings that received heavy damage by enemy rockets and mortar fire. The clay-tiled roofs, after being exposed to this fire, were particularly difficult to walk on. (Dix collection)

The road to the PRU camp, where the Pilatus Porter landed to drop us off after the trip to Can Tho. (Dix collection)

The Caribou aircraft beginning it's drop of resupplies on the PRU camp. (Dix collection)

The resupply drop was right on the smoke. The aircrews were, without exception, extremely excellent. (Dix collection)

Awards and camp dedication ceremony at the PRU camp a few weeks after the TET offensive. (Dix collection)

The author, center, with Dick Flashpoler, on the right and Dennis Tolibas in front of the Provincial Senior Advisor's house the day following the re-capture of Chau Phu. (Dix collection)

A few days following the TET offensive, the author is passing out small gifts to the "Heroes" of the battle. Note the pride on their faces! Maggie is in the rear observing the ceremony. (Dix collection)

Author, left and Jim Monroe with captured enemy weapons. (Dix collection)

The Province Chief pinning a Cross of Gallantry on Jim Moore, aka, Jim Monroe. The author is to the front. (Monroe collection)

HONOR MEN — President Johnson pre-
sents the Medal of Honor to Army Staff
Sgt. Drew D. Dix of Pueblo, Colo., the

fourth to receive the award in a ceremony at the White House. Others are (left
to right) Navy Lt. Clyde E. Lassen of

Englewood, Fla., and Marine Maj.
Stephen W. Pless and Air Force Lt. Col.
Joe Jackson, both of Newman, Ga. —AP

The author at the White House ceremony being awarded the Medal of Honor by President Lyndon B. Johnson. It was the last official act by the President before leaving office two days later. This ceremony was a joint service ceremony with, from left to right, Lt. Clyde E. Lassen, US Navy, Maj. Stephen W. Pless, US Marine Corps and Lt Col. Joe M. Jackson, US Air Force.

The inside of the CORDS office. Note the rear wall blown out! (Maggie O'Brien collection)

Jim Moore, aka, Monroe, with the radio, the author in the rear talking with one of the Nungs over a map. (Maggie O'Brien collection)

Maggie in front of the Chau Doc hospital taken a few days after the offensive. Note the bandaged left knee. (Maggie O' Brien collection)

The author reloading the fifty caliber. (Maggie O'Brien collection)

One of the buildings occupied by the VC. Note the contrast between this building and the one next to it. (Maggie O'Brien collection)

Westy on the left; Jim Lewellen, Jim Moore's replacement; center, the author on the right, a few months after TET. Taken just inside the Embassy House compound. Note the metal gates. (Maggie O'Brien collection)

The author getting ready to go out with the PRUs after Tet. (Maggie O'Brien collection)

One of the buildings occupied by the VC that they didn't want to leave without a fight! (Maggie O'Brien collection)

I started to hoist myself up onto the roof to reinforce my point. As I did, the Vietnamese girl came over and humbly interceded. I hadn't realized how intimidating the PRUs were to the average citizen. She began to speak softly to Tran and he obviously became agitated with her. He raised his voice and she cowered. I called down to her to speak to him.

"Go ahead, Co (Vietnamese for miss), it's OK. Tell him what I plan to do."

In just a few moments, she got the message across and Tran barked orders for some of his men to get on the roof and to go with me. The truck had been parked just under the overhang. Four men hopped up on to the truck and continued to the top before I could turn around and climb up there myself. There they waited for me.

When I reached them, they handed me four grenades. I put three into my pockets and pulled the pin on one and tossed it toward the rear of the compound. This was the signal for them to start firing.

Without delay, I jumped down on to the boxes which were against the wall. When I dropped onto the cement floor, I turned toward the main building, following the instructions that the Filipinos had given me. Not wanting to waste any time, I just sprinted across the compound courtyard stopping at each corner and tossed a grenade around the corner.

I spotted the back entrance to the main office building. Two VC ducked into it and immediately returned fire from the open doorway. A squad-sized unit was moving to the rear of the compound near a small clump of hedges. These two in the doorway seemed to be covering their withdrawal. When they ducked back to reload, I tossed my last grenade into the room with them. Not hearing any more from them I rushed the room.

I must be in the right room. This looked like a major office as I stumbled over broken furniture and two dead VC. Not being able to see due to the cloud of dust from my grenade, I crouched down to look under the smoke and spotted the safe in the middle of the room. I ran to it and saw that it hadn't been disturbed. I turned to leave just as three VC entered the room from a hole in the east wall less than 20 feet away; but they didn't see me because of the smoke. I fired on them with my Swedish-K, killing two. The third one yelled and ducked back into the hole in the wall like a rat. Just as he did, I could hear the bolt of the Swedish-K fall on an empty chamber. I quickly pulled the old magazine out and dropped it to the floor and slapped my last one in to the weapon.

It was time to leave this place. The longer I stayed, the dumber the idea of going back in there seemed. I turned to exit and out of the corner of my eye I spotted a real survivor: A full bottle of "Old Crow" whiskey perched on top of a tall cabinet. I ran over, snatched my prize and tucked it into my camouflaged fatigue jacket.

Without further delay, I ran to the wall as the PRUs let loose a heavy volume of covering fire just over my head. In three jumps I was over the wall. I was getting used to this climb and once more I shuddered as I realized that I was setting up another pattern. Now it was time to get out of here.

I ran by my covering element and they quickly followed me off the roof and down onto the street. Time was wasting and I knew we had to get moving. Seeing that I was not injured, everyone seemed noticeably relieved. Dennis and Arturo ran over and literally hugged me. I handed Arturo the bottle I pulled from my jacket. "Have a drink for your eye," I told him.

I smiled at Dennis and said, "You can have one too. It will settle you down." He grabbed the bottle, took a long pull and handed it back to me. Then I passed it to the PRUs and it was gone in seconds.

I looked up and the Vietnamese girl was looking a bit embarrassed as some of the PRUs were pointing something out to her. They all began pointing at me. I looked down to see what was so funny. At least, I guess it was kind of funny. The entire inseam of my pants was split. The only place it was still attached was about an inch or so on each leg at the cuff. I had to admit I must have looked pretty stupid with my balls hanging out.

Up to this point, I was wondering how I was able to get the drop on the VC at a couple of critical moments. It was clear now. They no doubt were too shocked at seeing this American running around with his nuts hanging out!

Tolibas and Gatpayat muffled a laugh; but when they saw that I was willing to laugh it off, they each let out a roar. Obviously they were relieved that they were getting out of this place.

"All right," I yelled, half laughing, but still serious. "Let's get out of here. Di di mau, God damn it."

We weren't out of the woods yet.

"We go Embassy House," I said to Tran, who was still amused at my situation and making some obscene comment to the young girl.

Suddenly, out of the corner of my view, I caught sight of movement at the same time I heard Vietnamese voices. I grabbed Tran's arm to get his attention. I cupped my right ear and said "VC." He immediately responded by ordering his men to get down. Then we saw a squad-sized force shuffling along the street about two blocks away. We watched as they disappeared around the corner in the direction of the theater.

"No shoot!" I whispered. "We go," and I gestured toward the TOC. Everyone in the group was still pumped up from our tremendous success but all seemed relieved at not having to pursue the VC again right away.

It looked to me as if the VC were regrouping. The manner in which they were moving and just before dark indicated to me that they were probably consolidating their defensive positions for the night. I was sure that they probably didn't know much more about us than we knew about them. I still didn't know what the enemy strength was but figured it was significant. The permanent enemy strength operating throughout this province was three battalions. There was the 510th, the 512th and the Muy Tre. So far I hadn't identified elements of any of the three. There were also a few enemy units operating from Cambodia which could easily support a major offensive like this. In any case I didn't want them to know there were only about 15 of us.

Most likely they knew an American unit was present since they surely heard the SEALs earlier. I was certain they didn't know what size American unit was in the fight, but it might keep them guessing and their confusion put us on more equal ground. I sure as hell didn't want to get tied up with an unknown enemy unit that clearly outnumbered us in the streets of the city after dark. I liked the night but preferred the bush to the streets.

We climbed in to the Ford and headed for the TOC. I called Jim on the radio so he could let Major Phoung know that we were on our way back. We still had a couple hours until dark but didn't need any more trouble now. I also told Jim that we were bringing the two Filipinos back and one Vietnamese girl, also a CORDS employee.

We had been extremely lucky with only three PRUs wounded, one SEAL slightly wounded and Ted, who I didn't expect to make it. I only had a few bruises here and there, a split lip caused from falling through the roof and, of course, my embarrassment from exposing myself to the world. Despite Ted's serious condition, we had been lucky considering the gravity of the overall situation in Chau Phu.

Our trip back to the TOC was uneventful. The activity in the downtown area had quieted down significantly. A couple sniper rounds hit the street to our front and a couple zipped overhead. None provoked a response from our force as we worked our way through the streets. In the distance I could hear heavy mortars. It sounded like it was coming from the western approach to the city. There were no friendlies in that direction except for the district headquarters at Tinh Binh. I knew some of the American advisors from that camp about 20 miles down the road and toward the Vinh Te canal. They were a good bunch of guys. I knew that if they weren't up to their ass in alligators, they would try to get to us.

I could sense the pride my troops had, and I must admit I was feeling kind of good too. No doubt the PRUs would again rub it in when they got to the TOC. I wouldn't blame them. After all there hadn't been much support from the local Vietnamese since the offensive started. The only exception was the small group of police who secured their headquarters. I wondered if they still had control of it and if they'd make it through the night.

One master sergeant I'd gotten to know fairly well when I got the two .50-caliber machine guns I ordered through our channels. I had some difficulty getting them timed to fire correctly. Master Sergeant Williams helped me service them and gave me a quick refresher class on timing of the weapon.

Prior to deployment to Vietnam, my A-Team had extensive cross-training from our weapons specialist on almost every U.S. and most foreign weapons commonly used in this theater of operations. I probably fired over a thousand rounds of .50-caliber for familiarization on the multi-weapons range at Fort Bragg. I must have missed the class on maintenance or was more interested in firing them. In any case, Sergeant Williams was an expert on the .50-caliber and shared this love affair he had with it with me. I had ordered three .50s and had loaned him one since the Americans didn't have any major firepower under their control, and the camp situation was a bit tenuous because of the tension between the Vietnamese command and their advisors.

That's the way it was in some camps in the Delta. It seems that when some of the former U.S. Special Forces camps were turned over to the Vietnamese, there was an effort by the Vietnamese to try to take complete control of the operation. Either they were trying to prove they could run things or they were influenced by the Viet Cong. Whatever the reason was, it was not a good situation and I felt the least I could do was help with firepower. After all, our program had a generous budget. We could get virtually anything we needed and I could easily replace the .50 if we needed another one.

I actually enjoyed the quiet ride back and began to reflect on the progress we had made. I felt good about it and started reconstructing the day's events. I thought about the .50 going out of time again earlier in the day and wondered if we had an ammunition problem or was it a maintenance problem. Whatever it was, I'd be able to work on it later that night if the SEALs had brought it back to the compound.

We stopped by the TOC and as before, the gate swung open automatically. I sent my two casualties to join the other one with the weird head wound to get medical attention. I was sure Major Phoung had a medic close by.

I told Tran that we would leave in 10 minutes for the Embassy House. First, I needed to talk with Major Phoung. I found him in the radio room talking with the Tinh Binh district headquarters. He was yelling into the radio in Vietnamese something about they needed to try to get to the TOC before night.

Upon seeing me, he put down the handset and instructed one of his captains to keep up the pressure on the Tinh Binh force to get into the city to help him. They apparently had been trying to get here since early afternoon. The heavy mortars and automatic-weapons fire I had just heard was them bogged down at the edge of town.

"Thieu ta, Phoung?" I asked. "What is the situation? Has it

changed since I left you this afternoon?"

"No, Drew. We still only have about 50 men here and no rein-forcement can come. The VC blow the bridge into town. The big bridge on the road to Tinh Binh."

"Yes, I know the one. Where are the troops from Tinh Binh?"

"They are now trying to go around the bridge and come to us."

"Do you know if the American advisors are with them?"

"Yes, one maybe two now. Before there were more."

"What happened?" I cut in.

"One man killed."

"Who?" I asked.

"I don't know but I think it was the sergeant."

"Aw shit!" I sighed. He must mean the senior sergeant when he said "the sergeant." That's got to be Williams I thought. Damn he was a good guy. I never really felt that the advisors in Tinh Binh had much control over the situation and I could see them trying to get to Chau Doc without much help from their counterparts.

"Major Phoung," I asked, "what are the Tinh Binh units doing now?"

"They go back to District Headquarters tonight. Tomorrow they try to come again."

"OK, Major. I'm going to go to the Embassy House tonight and help defend them."

"Can you stay with us?" Major Phoung pleaded.

"No, I will take the PRUs and go."

"Leave the PRUs," he half ordered and half pleaded.

"No, Major, they go with me."

Hearing that, he turned and went back to the security of the radio room without a word.

"Major," I called after him. "Did you know that a few of your men took the Police Headquarters back from the VC?"

"No," he said and continued on into the radio room.

Oh well, I thought, and walked over to check on my men at the temporary aid station that was set up under a large shade tree at the far end of the compound.

I didn't have to understand the words to know they were really giving the Vietnamese a lot of shit about being holed up in the TOC. The PRU with the spectacular wound to the head was really pouring it on. I wished I had a better grasp of the language. I would have given a month's pay to know what was really being said.

"Let's go," I said in Vietnamese and pointed south toward our camp and the Embassy House. I really wanted to get back and see what the situation was there and I needed to turn the Filipinos over to Jim. There more than likely would be an assault on both places during the night.

If the VC knew that we were the ones responsible for kicking them out of the CORDS compound and annihilating at least one of their platoons, they would be on us for sure. If they were smart, they'll hit us hard. Maybe they'll attack the TOC. The Vietnamese would deserve that; then maybe they would get into the fight. My thoughts were generated by frustration and the fact that the outcome still was very much in doubt.

Without another word, all of my men quickly scrambled into the Ford, including the wounded. They obviously didn't want any part of this place. The VC probably would hit it after dark and from the looks of their defensive organization, the VNs wouldn't last long against an organized assault.

I called Jim on the radio to let him know we were on our way back and to expect us in about 10 minutes. The grossly overloaded truck quickly covered the distance to the front of the hospital.

Without warning, the driver suddenly slammed on his brakes and all of the PRUs jumped out of the vehicle. Half set up a hasty defensive position and the other half laid down their weapons and started dragging limbs and debris from the road. This maneuver was no doubt pre-arranged. I jumped out and helped the closest ones manhandle a heavy limb off the road.

In 20 seconds or so the VC realized we were there and the PBRs weren't around to support us. All hell broke loose as we made it back to the truck.

One PRU was hit in the foot and started to collapse immediately. His buddies, running along side, grabbed him before he actually hit the pavement. The round broke his ankle and bone was protruding from both sides of it. As soon as the last man was barely on board, the truck was in motion. A B-40 round passed over our heads and fell into the river. Everyone in the back of the truck was firing all weapons on full automatic.

As soon as we reached the end of the main street only 200 yards away, the firing dropped off completely. We were now heading down the narrow road that led to the Embassy House.

The layout of the town required that we go the same way each time. This made our movement completely predictable. It was still early but I began to think of our security for the night as we neared the compound.

None of the many small hooches on the approach to our place had been cleared so far. They could, more than likely, be used as jump-off positions for an attack against our compound. The locals definitely would know if that was in the works. One thing certain, they knew more than what they were letting on. I needed to get some feelers out and see what was going on.

The villagers certainly didn't want an assault to take place. If one did, many would be killed or wounded in the crossfire. We'd get the word out when I got back. The PRUs would be the perfect ones for that job. They didn't mess around and when they spoke, people usually listened! They had a way of making the risk seem very obvious. If the people were told that if they helped, we'd be able to protect them.

Siew, or Baby Face, as we called him, was the Nung on duty when we arrived. He called to one of the other Nungs to open the gate since he didn't want to vacate his position. The driver of our truck pulled up to the compound and stopped. Arturo, Dennis, the girl and I hopped out.

I called for one of the Nungs who spoke a little Vietnamese to tell Tran to check the immediate area to see if the locals knew anything about the VC. I didn't want us to be caught by an enemy sapper unit staging in the houses around us. Sappers with satchel charges would play hell with us.

Maan came up and I conveyed to him my concerns. He quickly grasped the idea and started conversing with Tran. I waited to make sure Maan had the idea and Tran understood. When it looked as if Tran was responding favorably, I gave him a hearty shake on the shoulder and gave the rest of the PRUs a loud "numba one" and a thumbs up.

They had done a great job and knew it; but the job wasn't over and we would need to head back into the city. The VC had had their nose bloodied and now we had to go back and kick hell out of them again tomorrow.

After this morning, I started to feel good about my role with the PRUs. I was beginning to develop a better understanding of my troops. Sure, we had worked together in some pretty hairy conditions before, but that was usually on our terms. Now we were doing pretty damn well against bad odds and they hadn't let me down.

I walked back to the radio room and met both Jim and Westy coming out of the building.

"Drew, it's good to have you back," both men said as I walked up.

"The two Filipinos are up front with the good-looking Co I told you about. Mr. Tull will be glad they are safe."

"Tull is not in town," Westy said. "He was on leave for the holiday like most everyone else. I believe he is in the Philippines with his wife. Dick Flashpoler is acting Senior Provincial advisor.

"He already has the word about their rescue and is real glad that they are safe. Drew, you should brief him when you put your shit up. I know he'll want to talk with you. He's really glad that you and the SEALs were able to get the other civilians out too."

"Yeah, that was a bit of luck. So far we've had our share of good luck," I responded.

"How many PRU casualties did you have?"

"Only three. What about Risher," I asked?

"I don't think he made it. Maggie was with Doc and they both worked on him doing everything they could. Maggie said that they put a tracheotomy in but said that it didn't look good at all."

"Yeah, I know, Jim. I really didn't think he would come out of it. He had a bad head wound." I added, "I'd hate to think how he would have been if he had survived."

"Yes, we saw him before he was put on the boat. Some of the SEALs are down-river securing an LZ for the Medivac and some are on the river," Jim volunteered.

"When will they be back and where are the others?"

"I'm not sure when they'll be back," Jim said. "Probably sometime tonight or tomorrow. They won't be back until they take care of the medivac or send his body out.

"Drew, Marcinko seemed a bit shook up about the possibility of losing Risher. He said something about not losing anymore SEALs to sniper fire, that his guys were too valuable for that."

"Yeah," I replied. "I heard something about that back at the TOC right after he was hit. I can tell you both this. The entire platoon would have gone back with the PRUs and me if it hadn't been for the orders not to go back. Gordy and Rex even told me that if we got into a jam, they would be there in a flash regardless of orders." I knew they would have too.

# CHAPTER 8

## OUR FIRST NIGHT— WILL THEY ATTACK?

"Jim," I asked, "where are the civilians and Maggie now?"

"They are still on the river. I think the Navy will take them down-river to Can Tho in a day or so. In any case they are going to stay on the river until this blows over. Right now there isn't much of a hurry."

Westy responded, "Can Tho is still in pretty serious trouble of their own."

"Are they getting any reinforcements out to any of the hotspots?"

"No, Drew. So far it seems like everyone is still on their own. We can't expect any help here for a while," said Jim. "What does it look like in the city? I'd like to get a report to Saigon. They've been pushing the field units for a SITREP (situation report). Drew, from what I can make out on the radio, no one really knows the extent of this offensive."

"Well, Jim, I don't have a handle on it yet but from the number of crew-served weapons we are up against, mainly mortars, I'm sure we have elements of at least one main-force battalion committed to this attack.

"Jim, Westy, I'm certain that the attack was initiated from within the city limits. Early this morning, when we first arrived in town, all the enemy mortars were being fired from within the city. The gunners were close to the front. I bet the Vietnamese units really caught them by surprise."

"What do you mean Drew? Westy asked.

"Well from what I can see, the Viet Cong were prepared for a major attack on the city."

"Well, what do you mean, Drew?"

"I mean the Vietnamese defenders weren't there to resist and the VC moved in faster than they expected and probably out-ran their support. They were using mortars when they just needed to move in with direct-fire weapons like rockets.

"Hell, from what I've seen today, they missed their chance. If they don't push us tonight, they aren't going to succeed."

"Well I hope you're right, Drew. We don't have the means to put up a long fight," Westy said. "We could get low on ammo real fast. What about your troops, Drew? How are they on ammo?"

"They have a good supply at the camp. They could hold out for quite a while. I've got about 47 men with their families at the airfield camp. The rest are deployed at each of the districts and I haven't gotten a status report on them yet."

"Drew, what are your plans now?" Jim asked.

"I'm going to make a run to the camp. I should be back in 20 minutes or so. I want to see what Bao thinks. I'd like to get his idea on what the VC have in mind. He's the only one I know who really thinks like one. We also can give each other some moral support.

"I'll take my Jeep and two of the Nungs. Watch for us. We won't be sparing the horses on our way back. Have you seen any VC activity in that direction?"

"No and the SEALs didn't report any when they first went out to recon a possible LZ for the medivac. You better get moving, Drew, if you're going to make it back by dark."

"I'll have the radio." I ran to my room and picked up a fresh PRC-25 battery for the radio and found another pair of cammie pants (camouflage fatigues). I really wasn't in the mood for any more jokes concerning my anatomy. The troops had their laugh, but they had a way of not letting anything go when it involved me. I knew it was just their way of communicating with the boss.

I called for Nago to get me some more 9mm ammo. He had beaten me to it and was standing behind me with a fresh ammo bag full and a canvas bag with some grenades in it.

"Get one Nung and we go see Bao in my Jeep."

I was glad that the Jeep made it back. Nago already had reworked the timing on the .50-caliber so it was ready to go again. Nago was back in a flash with Lin. He threw in an 1897 pump-action 12-gauge and a canvas bag of shotgun shells loaded with fleshettes. Nago usually thought of everything and today was no exception.

The three of us climbed into the Jeep. Nago was on the .50 and Lin was serving as assistant gunner. I yelled for them to hang on as I floored the Jeep and turned left for the mile and a half run to the airfield.

I was glad that we had started construction of the camp. It was still somewhat makeshift as far as accommodations were concerned, but the fighting positions were in pretty good shape and that was all that mattered now. At least we had a secured area not far from the Embassy House as well as security for the airfield itself.

Even if the airfield was only partially completed, it was one of our options we had for an evasion plan if someday we ran out our welcome. This night just might be the night. An E&E (escape & evasion) plan is good practice for guys like us who always operate outnumbered and working with indigenous forces. Needless to say, our E&E plan was known only to the three of us.

Bao was on full alert. He had sentries positioned at key points along the route to the compound. I was sure he knew we were approaching. I had just supplied him with two PRC-25 radios. I knew he used them a lot because I could barely keep up with his battery requests.

I turned west onto the airport road just as we left the last little hooch on that side of the road. From there it was all open and very flat, exactly how you would think an airfield would look. The raised portion of the field itself was only about 300 feet long and about 50 feet wide so far. It was not yet suitable for large aircraft but good enough for the Pilatus Porter or Helio Courier to work out of for our operations. There were no trees on either end; so as long as they got their wheels up, they could make it fine.

The Vietnamese engineer unit assigned to provide gravel hadn't made as much progress as we would have liked. They seemed more interested in selling the gravel, which was extremely scarce in the Delta, on the local economy. This became a real sore spot with the three of us, but since I was mainly concerned with operations, I ignored it.

I guess I ignored it long enough until the rumors that "Pappy Johnson", a special forces sergeant from the B-Team, was on his way to Saigon to trade for his very own rock crusher. The rumor was enough to put a damper on the Vietnamese gravel business. That had just happened. So as not to lose all of their business, the Vietnamese started supplying the needed gravel and progress really picked up on camp construction.

Prior to having the airfield, we just had the Caribou aircraft, operated by Air America, land on the hard-packed rice fields in the dry season. During the rainy season, when the fields were flooded with about four or five feet of water, we had C-123's with Chinese crews from Taiwan airdrop our supplies at the same place, but in the water.

The camp was being constructed on a rectangular pad on one side of the proposed strip. So far the pad was about 80 yards square and only had the beginnings of two buildings on one side. The defensive positions were built on the side of the pad looking out over the flat rice fields. The idea was that very little of the camp was silhouetted against the sky, which made it hard for enemy gunners to hit.

It melded into the countryside. That worked real well until we started making a big dent in the VC infrastructure. I didn't want to waste manpower, first building the camp and then having to defend it once it was completed; but we had to do something because the PRU were being targeted more frequently because of the tremendous success we were having in eliminating the infrastructure.

Having a camp also took the pressure off the locals to house my troops. Forcing the locals to support us with shelter and food for long periods was beginning to have a negative impact on our operations. You can operate only so long by taking over a family's house and expect to be fed. We always paid for what we used when I was with my men; but because of the power thing in the Vietnamese culture, I knew damn well the troops didn't pay or not well enough for what they received.

It was taking a while for this to sink in but we were starting to get more positive feedback from the locals as a result of less pressure by us. After all we were probably no better than the VC under the old rule of "take it for the cause." In both cases the people probably only agreed because of fear. We weren't going to change the way of life but we would do what got us the best return.

Bao was waiting for us as we entered the camp. He always had a smile on his face whether he meant it or not. This smile was greatly enhanced by the full set of gold teeth in his mouth. He was in full leopard-spot fatigues, which was not normal for him. He usually wore black pajamas when around the camp as if he were always lounging. So I knew he thought our situation was serious.

He shuffled up to me and grasped my right hand with both of his and motioned me to his quarters. He barked orders out to his personal staff and they immediately reappeared with hot tea. I was glad he didn't serve the usual bottles of beer or brandy.

Bao spoke almost no English, which was surprising since he had worked so long with Americans. It was probably more a result of his character than anything else. He was a man in his upper 40s and highly respected by those under him and greatly feared by all the Vietnamese who didn't have his respect. I liked him and we had developed a strong mutual respect for each other earlier in my tour.

Soon after I arrived in the province, he made a run on me by intimidation. He wanted full control of the PRU. He sought full autonomy to run operations without my knowledge and wanted to go on his own and just report the results. That would have been disastrous. Combining their cultural tendency to control with the power that had been given us would have placed him in a position of tremendous strength.

Who knows what the final outcome would have been. Because of the increasing animosity between them and the Vietnamese authority, one thing I know for sure, the PRUs never would have given up their weapons and power without a fight, if and when this war ended.

When Bao made the serious run on me two months back, I had to take drastic measures to get his attention by confiscating all of the weapons from his men. Jim and I took the Nungs into his camp under the pretense that I was going to give them all new M-16's. When Bao suddenly realized what was happening, things got pretty dicey. The Nungs gradually positioned themselves at strategic locations while Bao's weapons were being tossed into the back of our two-and-a-half-ton truck. After a couple of tense moments with almost 100 feisty PRUs jockeying around with grenade pins pulled, we suddenly drove off leaving them standing there with only their side arms and a few crew-served weapons.

I heard Jim years later say, "That day was the hairiest day of my life!"

The next day Bao walked into the Embassy House and requested permission to speak with me. It was hard for a man of his stature and respect to do this but from where I saw it, he didn't have much choice. He agreed to play ball with me.

Of course I went out of my way and even a little overboard to help restore his respect. A few dollars raise for him and his men didn't hurt. And a huge party at the camp, where I provided a healthy supply of good brandy and beer, also did much to restore his status and re-establish the good faith between us.

The Embassy House had a respectable supply of booze just for occasions like this. It was well known that high-level Vietnamese liked to drink and party hardy. The booze in our storeroom was just for that purpose: A bribe to get favors from the local commanders, including the province chief. Jim and Westy didn't really believe in giving the booze away for that purpose. Jim, probably because he didn't drink and also because he didn't like to give them anything they didn't deserve. Westy, because he was tight with the money. As a result there was always plenty of good operational stuff on hand for us and in this case for the party.

It didn't hurt building Bao's respect either when I invited a few of the high-ranking Vietnamese to attend. They actually became offended when they found out that Bao had access to such a generous supply of really good booze. I loved it!

There was really no love lost between us and the province chief anyway and it was great to see him stew. It really got to him when Bao offered him a bottle of Napoleon five star as a gift that was easily worth $50 on the Vietnamese market. That was about a month's pay for a lieutenant.

After a few healthy drinks, Bao and I started dancing a jig with each other and doing the limbo. The troops loved it and from then on we were great friends. We would have many good times together throughout the countryside and many successful operations.

"Bao," I said, "many VC in Chau Doc."

"Yes," he answered and made a sweeping gesture with his arm in the direction of the city. I pointed to him and then to myself and said, "We kill VC." This he understood and gave a sly look as he drew his hand across his throat, which I understood completely. That was the extent of our conversation so I drank my tea and stood.

"Bao, I go to Embassy House," and pointed in that direction. He grinned as he barked out some orders to his men to escort us back. "Thank you," I said and walked over to Tran and gave him a hearty handshake. Bao knew what I meant and gave a thumbs up acknowledging my pleasure in Tran's performance earlier.

I pointed to Tran's head and shrugged my shoulders which was my way of asking how the man was doing with the unusual head wound. He understood and made a gesture that I understood to mean he was all right. At this, Bao laughed and shook his head. I said to Nago and Lin that we needed to go. Nago brought the Jeep over and we departed with our escort.

After we arrived at the compound, Jim asked me to go over the rooftop defenses with him, which I did. We walked up the back steps to the .50-caliber position. I was glad to see that Nago had secured the "go/no go tool" to the machine-gun mount. This was the standard tool used to set the timing of the .50. One way the timing was too tight, the other it was just right.

Nago made especially sure that we noticed the .30-caliber machine-gun emplacement. The Nungs had linked together a continuous belt of about 5,000 rounds and had them neatly placed in empty wooden 81mm mortar crates to keep them clean.

I told Nago to check the timing on the .50, which he indicated he had already done.

"Good man, Nago. Where are the grenades?" I asked.

Jim said, "You'll like this" as he walked over to the front of the roof and opened a crate loaded with 30 to 40 M-26 grenades unwrapped and ready. There were three similar crates, one at each section of the roof.

"Well, Jim, I guess we're about as ready as we can be."

Jim was a good operator and knew what needed to be done. I liked the way he always seemed calm. The Nungs liked him and watched out for him. Sure they knew he was the boss but they also knew he would watch out for them as well.

I went down to my room to get a few minutes sleep. I knew that it would be a long night even if the attack didn't come. Before I went into the room, I went to the main bunker in front. Two Nungs were inside in full combat gear, including flak jackets and steel helmets. I spoke a few words to them and then I went to the rear of the compound to check on the river position. Two guards were there as well.

There definitely was a tense feeling in the air. We all knew if the VC wanted this place, they probably could take it but they damn sure were going to pay big to do it. We were heavily armed and had a good supply of ammo in the compound if the ammo bunker didn't get hit.

One thing for sure, it was hard to hit the compound with indirect mortar fire because it was so small. The main thing we had to worry about was a sapper attack or direct fire weapons like B-40s.

I counted and determined there were more than one crew-served weapon for each of the 16 Nungs and the three of us. Also Nago had placed a 12-gauge 1897-pump riot gun at each shooting port with a claymore bag full of fleshette rounds, just in case a person was walking by when we were hit and he didn't have his personal weapon with him. Seeing that we were in about as good shape as could be expected, I went to get some sleep.

I had been lying down for scarcely 20 minutes when Westy started banging on my door. I had been listening to the rocket and mortar explosions to the west and wondering just how close they were. As Westy began knocking, the rattle of machine-gun fire was unmistakably close.

"Drew, get up. I think they're making a push."

"I'm awake," I called from a semi-conscious state. "I'm coming."

I reached up above my head and grabbed my shotgun and a bag of shells that Nago had prepared earlier. I already had my pants on and left the room without a shirt and ran up the back stairs to the roof. Two of the Nungs were already on the .50-caliber and were firing down the road toward the airfield. They stepped back for me to take over the gun but I gestured for them to continue.

I went to each position and checked the status of the weapons. Jim was crouched down behind the .30-caliber machine gun and assisted the Nung gunner with it. Two or three SEALs who had been left at the Embassy House while the others went down-river were manning crew-served weapons as well.

"Jim," I yelled over the noise of small-arms fire, "what's going on?"

"It looks like they tried to hit us from the south here," as he pointed toward the hooches. "I think they were going to use the civilians as cover but one of the Nungs on the roof spotted them moving down the road. I think we discouraged them because we haven't taken anymore fire since we first saw them."

"That was a stroke of luck," I replied. "If they ever get to us with a sapper squad, we're in trouble. They could take the wall out just below us and be in here in seconds."

"Right, Drew. Don't tell them or they'll try!"

To our right, the mortars and rocket fire I had been listening to while lying in bed were still going on.

"Jim, what's happening over there?" Answering my own question, I said, "I think the Tinh Binh district troops are either trying to make it into the city or they are pinned down from their earlier attempt. I told you that Major Phoung said that an American sergeant was KIA earlier today. It was probably William's.

"When I was in town with the PRUs, I thought I heard a .50 firing from that direction. I bet it was the one we loaned him."

"It probably was, Drew, I don't know of any other .50-caliber in this area being used by ground troops except for the VC of course."

We watched the explosions in the distance. They appeared like bright flash bulbs when they reflected off the scattered smoke layer that hung over the downtown.

I was glad we had given the Special Forces B-Team the 81mm mortar they were now using to illuminate the sky. Throughout the night we had been alternating firing flares to illuminate their camp and ours. We would fire one illumination round, wait for it to burn out and then they would do the same. That was the deal when I left the mortar with the weapons sergeant just two weeks earlier after they were rocketed from the noodle factory across the river.

I couldn't believe they didn't have mortars. It was a real shame because they had such talent there, such as the weapons and communications sergeants. I knew them from my training days at Fort Bragg; both were highly trained and had prior experience on A-Teams from previous tours in Vietnam. I remembered walking into the B-42 headquarters soon after arriving in Chau Doc and they both recognized me but neither acknowledged it. I was wearing civilian clothes and they weren't sure if they should. In those days it wasn't uncommon for Special-Forces types to be operating incognito.

I was trying to pinpoint the small-arms fire to get an idea where the enemy might be located when we went into the city tomorrow. Right now, it looked like the VC were near the Police Headquarters which the Vietnamese police squad had taken back when the SEALs and I were in there before.

I didn't think the police would be able to hold out. They probably were successful earlier because the VC were moving through and weren't ready to stay. I could tell from my position on the roof that if the green tracers were concentrating on the police station, they were hurting.

It looked like a VC company was having, what we called on the training range, a mad minute. That's when all the weapons you trained with were fired at once to give the defenders a feeling of what it was like. Sometimes it was used by defenders to impress an enemy force that might be contemplating an assault on your position.

In this case the VC were impressing us on the roof. I'm sure they had gotten the attention of whomever they were firing on. A stream of green tracers would shower down on the target, and it was answered by a puny response of red tracers from the defenders. Each time I saw that, a cold chill ran down my back. I could imagine what must be going through their minds as they no doubt were counting their rounds. I wished Major Phoung had sent troops into the city. Maybe they would have been able to take some of the pressure off those poor souls at the police station. We'd find out tomorrow.

"Drew, you've been up for a few days with little sleep," Jim said. "Get some rest. I'll wake you before they get over the wall."

"I'll do that," laughing at his bit of black humor. "I'm going to get word to the PRUs to come earlier tomorrow. We need to get an early start before daylight. I think I'll take my chances with the TOC. We should be able to get by them without an incident. I'm not sure if I want to tell them our plans."

"Drew, you are a suspicious son of a bitch but you're probably right," Jim replied.

I went to my room but not before I had one of our Vietnamese interpreters send word on the radio to the PRU camp to come early. I had him talk around the subject as much as he could and not completely lose the point. I thought it sounded like the message got through but I cringed when they started the conversation.

Vietnamese whistle in the microphone before they talk. It seems they don't believe it's working or something. Maybe 10 years ago one Vietnamese was training someplace and the instructor did that and the word got out that was the only way to make it work. They also have a hard time talking low or in a whisper because their language is 90 percent tonal. Without inflections in their voice, they might say a number of different words since many are spelled exactly the same. Whatever the reason, it was amusing at times hearing them try to whisper.

# CHAPTER 9

## "NUMBA ONE" VC — A BIG BREAK

It was just after 0400 hours and the mortars and rocket fire had been quiet for almost an hour. All I could hear now was the isolated report from a sniper's weapon. The assault on the Police Headquarters had long since died down. The Special Forces troops at B-42 were putting up only an occasional hand-held flare, probably trying to conserve the 81mm flares for a time when they were really needed.

The attack on Chau Phu was beginning its second 24-hour period. Soon we would know how much real estate the VC had gained during the night.

The Nungs were stirring around outside. I could hear someone going from position to position, probably serving hot tea and something to eat. The Nungs stayed in their positions all night. I couldn't sleep and spent most of the night, as did Jim and Westy, moving between the roof position and the rear guard position on the river.

While back there, I could see the PBRs moving silently up and down the river in back of the Embassy House. I admit that they looked awfully good just cruising in the shadows and waiting to strike. I'm sure they were keeping the VC from hitting us from that direction.

I walked up to the front guard position to see Nago and Maan and remind them that the PRUs should be coming soon. Maan was already on the alert for them.

"Hi, Nago, hi, Maan, not too many VC now. Maybe VC come in one or two hour," I said for conversation sake.

"Yes, sir," they both replied.

A hand-held flare fired from the roof of our compound popped overhead, lighting the road up from the south. I could make out the pick-up coming toward us. We all waited in silence as the truck slowly made its way until it stopped in front of the gate.

This time Phat was the senior man. The pick-up wouldn't fit in the compound, so I told Nago to tell the PRUs to leave the truck outside and to come in and wait for me. I left them to go find Jim and Westy.

Both were in the kitchen. Westy was cooking eggs and bacon for us and Jim was sitting at the table smoking a cigar.

"I'm going to take off with the PRUs in a few minutes," I told them. "They are outside in the truck now."

"Do you want some breakfast before you go?" Westy asked as he entered the room with a plate piled high with scrambled eggs and bacon.

"Yeah, sure," and I scraped a healthy portion off onto my plate.

Co Tu, our housekeeper and cook, obviously hadn't made it to the house yet. She lived in one of the small hooches less than a 100 feet to the south of us. I'm sure she thought she was better off not connected with us if the VC were successful in over-running our compound. She'd wait to see how things went. I really couldn't blame her and Westy was doing a good job filling in as the cook. I wolfed down the eggs and bacon as I briefed both of them on my plans. I really didn't have much of a plan except to get to the center of town with whatever number of men Bao sent.

"Jim, I hope to find some other ARVNs (Army of the Republic of Vietnam) holed up in the city and get them going. We can't possibly kick the VC out of town with 15 or 20 men. Even if we are successful in routing them out of key buildings, we need somebody to hold the positions we take. It will be like slapping a bucket of water. They just get displaced somewhere else."

"Good luck on that, Drew," Jim said. "I can't see anything like that happening. You're probably right but if we can hold out until some reinforcement can get to us, maybe we won't have to E&E out of here.

"Drew, if Westy and I are gone when you get here, we'll be on the river in the Boston Whaler."

Westy said something about destroying some of the piasters he had. Jim wasn't too keen on the idea and indicated to Westy that he thought destroying money was a little premature.

"Just take the initial precautions with the safes," he said to Westy. "We have some thermite grenades we can put on the safes if we have to leave in a hurry."

I interrupted saying, "OK, I'll stick with the PRUs and link up with you later if you're not here when I get back."

That being said, I finished the last of the eggs and bacon and moved out. Stopping by my room, I picked up two fresh PRC-25 batteries and my Swedish-K and a fresh pouch of magazines.

The PRUs were in the front of the building just inside the big metal gate. They all stood and acknowledged me but the enthusiasm of the previous day was gone. They were just like a group of migrant workers waiting before light to go out to work in the fields after too much celebration. I knew they were equipped for battle even if they weren't yet mentally prepared. Each carried a good double-load of ammo and at least six grenades apiece tied to their web gear. It was a good thing we were riding, I thought, they wouldn't make 100 meters on foot with the load they had. One carried our M-60 machine gun and everyone had at least 75 to 100 rounds of linked 7.62 ammo over their shoulders.

I was glad that one man carried an M-79 grenade launcher. He was the only one who didn't have extra M-60 ammo but made up for it with a special vest that carried 36 40mm rounds sewn in special pockets in the front and several more sewn on his back. The vest looked a lot like oversized shotgun shells lined up in neat rows all over his upper torso. I made a mental note not to sit next to him on the truck.

I gave a good pep talk which I knew they didn't understand but I hoped they got the message anyway. They had a right to be a tad nervous but didn't let it show. A few smiles and a bit of chuckling erupted, as I attempted more Vietnamese than I should have. Whatever worked, I thought, to get the momentum going.

The Nungs opened the gates for us and when we piled onto the pick-up, I counted 12. Jim met us and said he heard from the SEALs. The others were still down-river but would be back sometime soon.

"They'll be good to have at the House," I told him. "I'll keep in touch by radio and let you know what's happening."

"Take care, Drew. We'll be standing by the radio."

With that I told the driver and Phat, "Di di. Let's go kill cong." I yelled out the open window so the guys in the back could hear. They answered with their own versions of a charge. The driver floored the big Ford and didn't slow down for the hospital or the TOC. If there were VC in the hospital, we caught them by surprise. It was another 45 minutes before daylight.

I guess the ARVNS recognized the truck or Bao told them we were coming because we had a major reception lined up on the wall as we sped by at 60 miles an hour. The relatively small number of defenders were actually hanging over the wall and on the rooftops within the compound. They cheered and some fired their weapons in the air. How stupid, I thought, all this enthusiasm and none willing to use it to attack the enemy themselves.

We made the first turn without slowing down and I thought for sure the vehicle would tip over. The men in the back of the truck were holding their fire until we were fired upon in hopes that we would gain another foot of surprise. Each second that went by without being confronted would get us that much closer to our objective. Another right turn and we were within sight of Maggie's house. As soon as it came into view we started receiving sniper rounds. The driver started to zigzag in the street as if that would make us more difficult to hit. He must have seen too many war movies because I always felt the shortest distance between two points was a straight line. Maybe it worked because we made it through the first block under fire without a hit.

The second left turn was a different story. As soon as we made that turn, all hell broke loose. We were met by the unmistakable rattle of a light machine gun.

Our driver pulled up onto the curb and slammed on his brakes. I swung the passenger door open and Phat and I slid out onto the street and rolled toward the cover of the closest building. The rest of the PRUs immediately began to return fire and each scrambled to find his own cover.

Phat yelled something to his men and they immediately started to spread out and move away from the truck. I thought that was a hell of a good idea since the enemy still were concentrating their fire on the vehicle. Rounds were popping all around and I felt like I could single out each one as it struck the wall over our heads.

Both Phat and I looked at each other as we both heard the unmistakable woosh of a B-40. We rolled from out behind the vehicle as the rocket hit the building to our rear, scarcely 15 meters away. The PRUs looked good as they started maneuvering down both sides of the street. Our man with the M-79 grenade launcher was firing as fast as he could reload, directing the small deadly rounds toward their advance.

Most of the enemy fire was now coming from the first-floor windows and from the rooftops. A few individuals were on the street level and were firing over their shoulders as they ran ahead of us. We were making good progress but I was thinking that we might be moving too fast. The last thing we needed was to move past the VC and have them behind us.

I stopped momentarily with my back to the wall and Phat held up too. I wanted to explain my concerns to him about moving too fast but didn't want to take the time to do so. I just pointed up to a window behind me to indicate that there may be VC there. Coincidentally as I did, I saw a black pajama-clad individual dashed past the opening. I took the spot under fire and Phat yelled for two of his men to drop back and cover our rear. They both emptied their magazines at that window and as soon as they stopped firing to reload, an arm raised up and tossed out a hand grenade. Both PRUs saw it and fired a couple of rounds before they rolled away from the explosion.

One man rolled into the open sewage pit for cover. This 18-inch gutter was all that saved him. The grenade went off less than three feet from him. When the smoke cleared, he climbed out and started firing back at the window with a vengeance. He was covered with sewage and was really pissed off about it.

Meanwhile our element continued its advance. I had fired almost three 38-round magazines by then and began thinking that this was going to be a long day. As we moved closer to the police station, which was across the street to our front, the VC we were pursuing began to spread out to the left and right and disappeared down the cross street.

I passed my group and took a position on the corner of the building so I could peer down the street to my right and see if we were heading into an ambush. Looking toward the right I saw nothing; but to my left, I saw at least a platoon of men in fatigues move as a unit down the street and disappear into a cluster of residential dwellings not far to the left of the theater.

The theater was about two blocks to the southwest and just across the wide intersection which looked kind of like a traffic circle. That was going to be a bitch to cross, I thought, but it looked like the VC were using it as a major staging area for their offensive. From that location they could easily cover all movement in and out of the city center.

It was obvious now that the main objective for the offensive in Chau Phu City was to take and hold the town. They probably figured that because of its proximity to the Cambodian border, they might be able to hang onto it. That definitely would be a major psychological victory. Chau Doc has always been a contested part of Vietnam because it was a part of Cambodia at one time and many of the people were Cambodian as well.

Just as the enemy platoon disappeared, a vehicle carrying a few armed black pajama-clad men ground its gears as it moved away from us and disappeared down the road. It was headed toward the My Loc Hotel on the west edge of town. Obviously the driver wasn't familiar with his newly confiscated prize.

"Phat," I yelled and motioned for him to follow me to the other side of the street. I took cover behind the corner of the building and while on my belly slowly peered around the corner of the building. Sniper fire was still a threat but somewhat indiscriminate now. Phat actually laid on me as he also looked over my shoulder.

I pointed to the theater and said "maybe ba muoi, maybe bon muoi, VC," meaning 30 or 40, and pointed toward the theater. Phat responded with a "yaah, VC" and motioned that he agreed with me.

The Police Headquarters was just across the street to our front, maybe 30 meters or less. There was a wall around the entire police compound and from the looks of it there had been a hell of a lot of action there last night. Only a few square feet of the six-foot-high wall were left untouched.

About that time we both saw a few bandanna-clad foreheads bob around the top of the wall as if they were getting in position to fire at us. Phat shouted orders to the PRUs and they immediately opened up on the targets. For several seconds we exchanged fire with the enemy and it didn't seem like we were getting anywhere. We were actually in a bad position because the VC could fire down our street from behind the wall. Our M-79 was not able to do much damage to the wall and the overhanging trees within the police compound were detonating the rounds prematurely.

We were all firing on the VC except for the two Phat had directed to watch our rear. Then firing started from our rear and I knew we might be in trouble. About half of our force shifted their fire to the rear. I could see at least two positions that were firing on us. I alternated my attention between both directions but only fired at the wall to the front. I looked back for a third time and I caught a glimpse of what looked like four or five guys further behind the VC to our rear.

"Phat," I yelled. "Look, maybe PRU."

I pointed behind the attacking enemy and he saw the same four or five men wearing leopard-spotted uniforms. He leaped up, clearly exposing himself to the enemy fire, and got the attention of his men and told them that the PRU were there and to watch out for them.

I've often said that successful combat is nothing more than making the right move at the right time, hoping the enemy makes a mistake before you do, plus a hell of a lot of luck. Right now we were having a stroke of luck. The guys behind us had been shacked up, celebrating with their girl friends, since the attack had started. They saw us and decided to join in the action. Their timing was good for us but maybe not quite so good for them since they were being fired on initially by us.

The VC behind us started to panic when they realized they were now surrounded. They tried without success to seek cover by getting back into the buildings that were along the street. How quickly the tide turns. A few seconds ago, we were being assaulted from two sides and now they were in the same boat.

Finding that the doorways were locked, the VC frantically went from one to another. Seeing their predicament, the PRUs attacked in full force. All went in for the kill and in no time six enemy lay dead on the street. The victors hastily searched the bodies and, finding nothing of value except for their weapons, moved up to my position after they threw the captured weapons in the back of the pick-up. While this was going on Phat and I kept up the pressure on the enemy positions on the wall.

There were now 20 men with me, including the eight new ones. Things started looking up. If only some of the ARVNs would respond like the PRUs, we could take this town back.

I tried to reach the Embassy House by radio without success. The signal probably was blocked by the buildings.

After the others joined Phat and me, they laid a heavy volume of fire on the wall that faced us. It was a good 18 to 20 yards but I thought I could get a grenade over the wall and under the trees. I tried one and it hit the top of the wall and bounced halfway back to our position before it went off in the middle of the intersection. The second one just cleared the wall and as it exploded we rushed across the street without saying a word.

We caught our breath and rested against the wall to reload. A volume of fire came from within the compound but not directed toward us. The PRUs started yelling and immediately were answered by others.

The lieutenant who had taken the Police Headquarters yesterday had made it through the night with three of his men. All were wounded but managed to hide. Three were KIA and all would have been history if we hadn't made it back at first light. With the combined help of the four of them on the inside, we rushed the compound to clear it for the second time.

Phat and I sat under the tree to discuss our next move. The police lieutenant, who spoke a little English, joined us. The PRU medic looked after the wounds of his three men while the others scouted the area for VC stragglers and any weapons left by the dead.

I heard a couple of shots from one VC who wouldn't give up and the PRUs quickly silenced him. I wasn't too concerned that my men were killing prisoners because our business was to capture and they knew we gave a good reward for anyone taken alive. A live VC really would be handy now. We needed to find out what the main objective for this offensive was. I also desperately wanted to know the strength of the attackers.

One of the PRUs returned with papers taken off one of the dead officers. Phat couldn't read so I gave the papers to the police lieutenant. He looked up as he said, "This is from the 510th battalion. It say for him to attack at midnight and where must get food and ammunition."

"Does it say how many soldiers are to go with him and if other units are to join him in the battle?"

"No, sir, it say only what I tell you."

I gave the papers back to Phat, which he passed to one of his seconds for safekeeping.

"Ringo, Westhaven, over."

"Go ahead Westhaven. Anxious to get a progress report."

"Roger, Ringo. We have retaken the Police Headquarters and have four friendlies with us. They are wounded but we'll leave them here with some of my men to secure this place. I also have more of my troops that we linked up with." (I didn't want to give our strength over the net for obvious reasons.)

"OK," Jim said as he ended his conversation abruptly. I liked working for him. He had the self-confidence it took to resist asking a bunch of unnecessary questions as many commanders of lesser self-confidence would do. He left the decision-making to the one in the field who had the most knowledge of the situation. He also knew that if I needed anything, I would ask.

Seeing that we weren't going to find out anything from the dead ones and the document didn't have anything useful in it, I decided to keep up the pressure on the enemy. I told the lieutenant to tell Phat to leave some men here at the police station with him. We were going to go to the theater next.

The lieutenant didn't like the idea of being left twice, especially after the experience he and his men had had last night. I assured him that we wouldn't leave town without him but we needed to hold the places we kicked the VC out of so they wouldn't move back in. He understood completely and knew the situation was far from over.

I told Phat to position the M-60 at the corner of the compound to provide covering fire as we assaulted. He agreed and also gave special instructions to the M-79 man to cover us from the rear and for both of them to move up as we moved forward.

I was proud of the way the PRUs were performing. I had been in a number of small skirmishes with them in the past; and on a few occasions, when we were caught moving about, we successfully fought our way out. This was different though. We were in the biggest battle of our lives. We were vastly out-numbered and urban warfare can be the most brutal of all. So far we hadn't encountered many civilians. I wasn't sure why the VC hadn't used them as shields as they have done in the past in other places. The only reason I could think of was they wanted to keep on the good side of the local civilians for when they took over. Or maybe the town was theirs now anyway and they didn't need to use them.

"Let's go," I called to Phat and he relayed this command to his troops. We rushed the open area of the wide intersection. As soon as we reached the center, the VC opened up with small arms and B-40 rockets. Everyone dropped in place and returned fire. Phat shouted a series of rapid-fire orders to the M-60 gunner and the M-79 man to cover us. As soon as their fire was directed on the enemy positions, all of us continued our dash to the other side.

When I reached the wide steps of the theater entrance, I went to the left side to find cover from the enemy fire which had picked up as more of their troops were pulled into our sector. I could see that the majority of the fire was coming from the backside of the CORDS compound and down the street toward the My Loc Hotel.

The road to the My Loc was on the main entrance to the city from the west. In the distance I thought I could see the burned-out body of an M-151 U.S. Army Jeep. It probably was the one Sergeant Williams was driving, trying to get into the city yesterday to reinforce us.

I called to Phat for us to move around the theater on the left side. He quickly responded and his men followed him to my position. It seemed that the enemy was not on this side of the building. This side also had many residential buildings that I wasn't familiar with.

I knew that several VC were in the theater because I saw them go in the front door when we first assaulted the Police Headquarters. The side of the building we were on had a large exit door similar to theaters in the states. I motioned for Phat to send some of his men down to the end of the theater and cover us. We didn't need for the VC to come around and see us concentrated along the wall.

We then fanned out just enough to cover the first row of houses that ran along the road adjacent to the building. We were making a quick sweep of the area so we wouldn't by-pass any VC. Phat directed the men to do a rapid search. They were kicking open the doors and taking a quick look. There weren't many people in their homes—they had long since moved out.

I stayed with the rear element and provided cover fire for our group and backed up the search party. It was better to have Vietnamese- and/or Cambodian-speaking individuals confront the civilians first. That did much to hold the confusion down.

Phat moved to the large theater exit door. As soon as he cracked the door slightly, a horrendous volume of fire erupted from within the theater and he quickly pushed the door closed.

We had been making good progress with the search and I noticed an older man wearing brown pajamas and sporting a VC type haircut. As I ran past, I grabbed him by the shirt and pulled him out of the hole he was crouched in. He wasn't armed but he sure looked out of place, watching the action and not really cowering down like a civilian with the volume of firing going on at the time.

The PRUs kind of looked at me as if I was a little nuts dragging this old man along.

For a minute it seemed like the firing was dropping off so I went up to the theater door and opened it. Once again a large volume of fire erupted. It was pitch black in there. From the closed door we could hear what sounded like a reinforced platoon on full automatic.

Phat reached for the door and as he opened it, I ducked in with my prisoner, holding him by his shirt, presenting him in the doorway. For a good two seconds the firing stopped and we went inside. Three or four PRUs hurried in with me. As soon as we got in, we moved to the side of the theater out of the light from the door and crouched down and literally holding our breath as we tried to get our night vision.

The PRUs outside got the idea and they propped the door open to keep light in there and stepped out of the way. There was sporadic fire from the enemy. I could tell the distinct sound of the AK-47 mixed with the smaller report from our 9mm and .30-caliber carbines. We were in a bad situation and we had to do something quick.

I remembered the firing stopped when we first opened the door, so I held up the old man once again. As his face hit the faint ray of light from the open door, the firing abruptly stopped. Seizing this opportunity, the PRUs immediately began yelling instructions. Soon I could hear the sounds of hardware hitting the cement floor.

Christ, I thought, they are throwing their weapons down. In no time we had the prisoners out in the daylight and lined up along the side of the building.

I knew we had a high-ranking prisoner and needed to get him back to the Embassy House as soon as possible. We were still heavily engaged but had to take a chance to break contact and get him back. I didn't like the situation we were in and it wasn't going to be easy, but this prisoner was worth the risk.

The entire country was engaged in a major offensive and this guy might shed some light on the overall VC objective. None of us at the Embassy House had any idea how widespread the offensive really was. Now we had almost 20 prisoners in addition to the 20 men we came with. I had a major logistical problem to deal with. How do I get all of us to where we needed to go?

We needed to get the pick-up from the Police Headquarters so we could put the prisoners in it. I didn't want to risk trying to herd all of them across the open area of that intersection. We would have enough trouble getting ourselves through that no man's land. First gesturing toward the truck still at the police compound and then to the prisoners, Phat picked up on my idea immediately.

He shouted instructions to his guys, and one immediately ran to the corner of the building where he could see the police compound. Through a series of hand signals, he relayed our orders. I wondered what the guys, in the security of the walled police compound, must be thinking about these orders. They surely had to be questioning the sign language. They easily could have denied being able to understand what was trying to be conveyed.

I immediately apologized mentally for my thoughts in doubting their courage. For up until now they had performed as well as any unit I had ever served with.

I heard the truck motor racing from inside the compound. Instantly the enemy small-arms fire shifted from us to the truck as it cleared the front gate of the compound. The truck raced straight for the wide intersection, obviously not concerned with the normal direction of traffic, it hopped over the curb on the edge of the intersection. I was sure the frame would come apart as it left the ground.

Small-arms fire hit all around the vehicle and bits of concrete sprayed the sides of the truck. Without slowing down, it hugged the side of the theater all the way to where we were waiting. The driver joined Phat at the front of the truck as soon as he shut it down and jumped out.

The driver was excited about something and shouting at a high-pitched rattle as he attempted to explain what had happened. It took four of us to pry open the hood since it was jammed pretty bad. After several attempts, we finally got the hood up. I was surprised at what

I saw. A number of new bullet holes were in the grill and the right side of the hood of the already battle-scarred truck.

The alternator was hanging loose and in two pieces. A round had gone through the right side of the hood and shattered the alternator housing. I thought it was hopeless trying to repair it here. The driver climbed in the engine compartment and started pulling wires from other non-essential parts of the vehicle like the headlights. In no time he jumped down from the engine compartment and said proudly "OK." Amazingly, he had wired the alternator housing together and with a clever knot cinched the two pieces tight.

I told Phat to load all of the prisoners into the truck and six of the PRUs. The rest of the men would join the others in the police compound and wait for us to return. It was obvious that the troops being left behind didn't like the idea but none objected. I said to Phat and so the others could hear, "We be back" and pointed to the ground "in ba muy phut." The round-trip shouldn't take more than 30 minutes and they should be able to take care of themselves for that amount of time. That is, I thought, if the truck doesn't give out in the process.

Phat remained with the stay-behind element and I climbed into the front seat of the Ford. I wasn't sure which of our two elements had the worst deal. The stay-behind element had to defend itself with a smaller force, but they would be in the compound. All they had to do was make it back across the no-man's land of the wide intersection one more time. On the other hand we had to enter the street from behind the theater and I knew as soon as we stuck our nose out into that traffic circle, we were going to be in a world of shit.

It took just a minute to decide that both elements would rush the intersection at the same time. The truck would be fully loaded with the prisoners and five PRUs in back and myself and the driver and one man in the cab. Twenty-five in the back seemed like a lot, but the

Vietnamese were fairly small and could really pack well.

My concern wasn't the load at all but the actual condition of the truck. It had sustained numerous hits over the past few hours and no telling what else was wrong with it. I couldn't imagine the alternator being able to withstand the bumps and jolts of the ride back.

The driver raced the motor as if warming up for the Indy 500. The second element moved to the front of the building and spread themselves out so they could all fire on the enemy. They waved to come ahead. The driver popped the clutch and the heavily loaded truck leaped forward. I glanced back for an instant and saw that the prisoners seemed a hell of a lot more nervous than the rest of us. I thought they must have a reason to be, after all they knew what their buddies had waiting for us.

As soon as the truck cleared the corner of the building, the firing increased from across the street. Our two guys with the M-60 and the M-79 grenade launcher began to place effective fire upon the VC positions as soon as the enemy exposed themselves. We had less than 100 meters to go until we reached the "safety" of the next street. It would help if the second element would rush now so they would draw some of the fire from us. I thought after all fair is fair!

The entire maneuver shouldn't take 30 or 40 seconds at most but right now it felt as if we were in a slow-moving dream. Come on, come on, I thought, as the vehicle moved toward the first buildings on the next street. Just then I could tell that the enemy fire had shifted, and I again mentally apologized for wishing the enemy would direct some of their fire onto the others.

I still can't figure out why the VC didn't commit their entire force to take the town. It was obvious they had enough troops for the job. To this point all we had to attack the enemy forces in the city were 20 PRUs, four police troops, the SEALs and the PBRs. All had been doing a tremendous job but in the overall scheme of things, we were a pretty small force.

I took the time to give the Embassy House a heads-up on our progress.

"Ringo, Westhaven, over."

As always, Jim was right there to answer as soon as the squelch was broken on the frequency: "Go ahead, over."

"We are on our way back to your location with some prisoners. Have any of our interpreters shown up yet?"

"Just the one we had earlier, over."

"Ringo, I think we have somebody worth talking with. We don't know who, but I just have a feeling."

"Roger, Westhaven, I'll get word to Bao, maybe they can get some information from him."

"Good idea," I said. "We'll be there in about zero five, out."

The driver put the truck in high gear as we went by the TOC and headed for the hospital. This time we didn't receive the expected small-arms fire, but I could see the destruction caused by the PBRs' .50-calibers.

Several dead VC could be seen laying in the front. That was odd, I thought; they always recover their dead when they can. The VC must have given up this place or there weren't any left to recover the dead. The PBRs were just too much for them to handle.

It also was surprisingly quiet the rest of the way back to the Embassy House. We arrived and parked the vehicle in front of the gate. I told the PRUs to wait there while I went inside.

Jim and Westy met me as I entered the compound.

"What do you have, Drew," Jim asked?

"I'm not sure, but we have 20 prisoners and their weapons."

"Good work. Where is the guy you think may be important?"

"Outside with the PRUs," I said as I called to the Nungs to tell the PRUs to bring in the prisoner. "He's been real quiet and hasn't said anything to the PRUs. I don't think they believe he is anybody."

"Well, Bao is sending someone over from the camp. They should be here soon. They were on their way over for something else when we called them. I think Ba Hung is with them."

Ba Hung was a former VC general, captured earlier under Jim's direction. Ba Hung has been a big help in locating other members of the infrastructure. Usually high-ranking members of the infrastructure don't turn very easy. In fact they seldom do. The situation with Ba Hung was unique.

Some months back, Bao ambushed Ba Hung and his security force when he was coming across the border from Cambodia. He had been the target and, as always, care was taken to keep the target alive, But sometimes the VC put up a bigger fight than expected, especially when the man they are protecting is as high up as Ba Hung was.

The ambush quickly got out of hand and every one of the enemy was killed. At least that is what Bao first thought. After Bao's men searched the dead, they pulled them off the trail and were just going to leave them. One of the PRUs noticed Ba Hung barely move and groan. The PRU gave emergency first aid and quickly brought him back to Chau Phu for treatment. It seems that he was so grateful for the care that he became a valuable asset. In fact he accompanied us on many operations and proved extremely valuable in making quick field identifications of VC cadre and knew the danger areas, like mine fields, when we moved about.

The prisoner was sitting on the cement floor of the compound with his back to the wall. He just watched us; and if I hadn't suspected something different, I would have said he was probably just an innocent bystander, caught up in the action.

A few minutes later, Ba Hung walked through the compound gates with three PRUs from the camp. As soon as Ba Hung and our guest's eyes met, a look of futility came over the latter's face. Ba Hung immediately walked over to him and the man stood. They both started talking rapidly. Neither Jim, Westy nor I knew what was being said.

One of the Nungs who understood some Vietnamese said, "This guy, he a numba one VC" and pointed to the man who had just resumed his position on the floor. Ba Hung turned to us and said "Sau Be" and pointed to the man seated on the floor.

Ba Hung spoke absolutely zero English but his expression was enough for me. It was one of mixed feelings and he obviously was not so glad we had captured this man. He actually appeared to be somewhat hurt, seeing the man of this importance sitting on the ground. Perhaps it reminded him all over again how it felt when the PRUs captured him.

That was enough for me. After I put the scene together from the theater and saw the reaction on his face when he saw Ba Hung, I knew we had someone we needed.

Jim, without hesitation said to Westy, "We need to get him to Can Tho or to Saigon."

"Right," Westy said. "I'll arrange an aircraft from Can Tho if they can get one here."

Westy turned and hurried off to the radio room.

"Jim," I said, "the rest of the PRUs are at the police station and we need to get back right away. When are the SEALs due back?"

"I don't know. I thought they would have been here by now. The last I heard, they were coming in this afternoon."

"OK. I'll go on downtown without them. I hope this guy can shed some light on the magnitude of the offensive."

"Yeah, Drew, it looks like he's what we have been looking for."

Just then Westy, hurrying back from the radio room, called to us: "Jim, they can send up a Porter from Can Tho tomorrow morning. It will be here about 0800 hours. I told them to land on the road and not to over-fly the city."

"Good idea," Jim replied.

"Jim, what do you think about me going with them to Can Tho?" I asked. I had quickly calculated that I could be back to Chau Doc in four to five hours.

"Yeah, Drew, I think you should. If this guy is as important as it looks, then we can't afford to lose him now. If things settle down around here, I'll go with you."

I turned to the PRU and motioned that I needed to tell him something. Not seeing our interpreter, I asked one of the Nungs who spoke English to translate to him that we would take Sau Be to Can Tho tomorrow.

The PRU started to turn. I grabbed his shoulder and said in just a couple words that they had done a really great job. A big smile came across his face.

"Oh, Maan. Tell him also to take the prisoners, including Sau Be, to the camp and keep them there. Tell him that the aircraft will land on the road tomorrow morning, not far from here but we need for the PRU to secure the area the plane will land."

I was really pushing it to expect Maan to be able to get all of that across. It took almost five minutes to translate. I was hoping the message got through. I was sure that most of it did and looked at Jim for his concurrence of what I was orchestrating. I knew once the prisoners were in Bao's hands, they would be secure. There was no way he would let that "prize" out of his control. Jim and I went into the house and sat down to go over the day's events while I waited for the PRUs to return.

# CHAPTER 10

## ARE THEY FINISHED?

"What do you think, Jim? Are they finished or are they going to continue the attack?"

"It's anybody's guess, Drew. I can't believe the VC haven't been able to cut us off and keep you contained in one place. You've been able to move freely, back and forth. They could easily have stopped us by blocking one of the key roads with debris or abandoned vehicles. We would have been screwed."

"Well, Jim, I don't think we're out of the woods yet."

On that note, Jim said, "We still have our E&E plan and we'll use it if we have to."

I left Jim to re-supply myself with a few fresh magazines and a couple of grenades.

Jim met me at the gate and asked, "Where to now?"

"The PRUs who are with me now are going to go back to the city and see if we can clear the hotel. That seems like the key enemy strong point now. When we were in town earlier, it seemed like most of the fire came from that location. If we can get them out of there, then we can control the high ground."

"Watch your ass, Drew. It's still pretty hot down there. The B-Team still hasn't been able to get out. I can't get much out of the colonel either."

Jim appeared really annoyed with that situation.

"Drew, some of the Special Forces personnel at the B-Team were trying to get out and help with kicking the VC out, but their commander wasn't hearing any of that. He confined all of them to their compound."

"What can I say, Jim? That's their problem."

"I know it, Drew, but God damn it, I wish they were here to go with you," Jim added, as I went through the gates.

"See you later. I've got the radio on our frequency. I'll call if I get into a jam and you can send Bao with help."

I climbed into my Jeep and two PRUs jumped in beside me. With me in the lead, the pick-up with the rest of my men headed back to the city.

It didn't take long to get by the hospital. We didn't receive any fire from there but noticed that the VC had removed their dead from the front lawn. Passing the TOC, we saw the same faces hanging over the wall. I thought they must be getting bored holed up in that place for more than 36 hours now. All they needed was some serious leadership and those troops would be great. After all, look at what the PRUs were doing and then there was the police lieutenant and his unit who prevailed over exceedingly bad odds. They hung in there until we arrived. I hope they are still in that compound with the other PRUs.

I didn't want to have to fight my way through that intersection again. That was the way the entire war was being fought. Take the ground. Then leave. Take it again! We may not win this war but we damn well were going to fight it differently in this province.

We could too. As Jim said, "We don't have a lot of politics to confuse the issue." He often equated our situation with the Old West. It was kind of wild and unruly and we were the marshals. Yeah, he was right, I was thinking as I passed familiar sites of recent shootouts; and like the Old West, the gunfighters were young, just like us.

The police compound came into view and as soon as it did, we started to receive small-arms fire from the street leading to the theater and the one to Major Phoung's house. As soon as we pulled up to the compound, the compound wall blocked us from the enemy view. I pulled my Jeep inside and left it there for the others to use to support us with the .50-caliber.

The police lieutenant, his men and the 14 PRUs were eagerly awaiting our return. I'm sure they were wondering what had happened to us since we said we'd be right back. Instead, we were gone for more than an hour. Phat looked a bit annoyed but restrained from saying anything to me. He did verbally assault the senior PRU with me, asking what had happened to us.

The man was somewhat forceful with his explanation, which was unusual within the PRU ranks. It was explained to Phat that I had to arrange to take Sau Be to Can Tho. Until then Phat hadn't realized the status of our prisoner. When he did, he relaxed immediately. In fact he took on an air of cockiness when he finally realized that he was partially responsible for the capture of someone with the equivalent rank of general.

"Phat," I said, interrupting the reunion with his troops. "we go now to movie."

I gestured toward the theater and then pointed to the re-supply of ammo the PRUs were tossing down from the pick-up. He was glad to get the re-supply because they were getting dangerously low. They hadn't had any major assaults to deal with during our absence, but did keep up a steady exchange of small-arms fire with the VC in the surrounding buildings.

I was hoping that the VC had forgotten about us being there but after hearing how Phat and his guys took on the VC snipers continuously since we had left, I knew they would be waiting for us when we left the police compound.

Fourteen PRUs were left at the Police Headquarters to hold on to that position. We needed a secure area to go to if we ran into trouble and they would be our reserve force if we needed one. The 57 recoilless rifle was left there but we took the M-60 and the grenade launcher. The machine gun was a little easier to move fast like we were about to do. We could always call for the recoilless if we needed it.

I was right. Just as the 15 of us dashed across the street, we took fire from several directions at the same time. We immediately fanned out and assaulted directly across the street with half the element and the other half with me followed the wall that ran along the police compound and headed directly toward the theater. The enemy fire was steady but in no way as intimidating as it had been earlier. It seemed like just enough to keep our interest up.

The volume of fire that we put out was considerably greater than theirs. Our man with the M-79 was obviously glad to get a re-supply of high explosive rounds and was using them as if there was no limit. Every dozen or so meters we ran, he would fire toward a window that looked like where a sniper might be hiding. I have to admit, he was good. Practically every round fell neatly into the open window, making it unlikely a sniper would survive.

When our two elements reached the intersection, we both rushed across at the same time. The enemy fire had dropped off enough, eliminating the need to fire-and-maneuver across. At least that was the reason I gave to myself. Ordinarily we would cover each other as we crossed the open area. In any case, we must have caught the enemy by surprise because they held their fire as if to let us cross.

As soon as we were in front of the theater, we turned to the right and headed down the street toward the My Loc Hotel. Very shortly, we started receiving a significant amount of small-arms fire. I wasn't sure what to expect. Very accurate mortar fire had to have been directed from the hotel. Since it was the tallest building around, it was the logical place for the VC to have a forward observer.

I wasn't sure what we were going to do after we got the VC out of the hotel, if we were able to. We didn't have enough troops to leave any there after we cleared the place. So far we had been able to pick up a few stragglers for that job, such as the unit we left at the Police Headquarters.

After moving a few hundred feet down the street, I could see two or three enemy on the roof of the hotel. No doubt they were the Forward Observers (FOs) who had been doing a great job of directing mortar fire on us and the rest of the city.

"Look, Phat! VC," and pointed to the roof of the hotel. I didn't have binoculars but from my position, it looked like the VC were watching us move toward them.

"VC see us," as I made a gesture by pointing to them and then looking through my fake binoculars made by the circles of my two thumbs and forefingers.

"Yaaah, VC look," Phat replied.

We needed to get moving before they could direct mortars or, worse, rockets on us. We were damn vulnerable sitting on the side of the street. We had enough problems with the snipers. We were on the south side of the street, which gave us the most concealment from the enemy FOs. If we could get a little closer, we probably could reach them with the M-79. Even within range I wasn't sure how easy it would be for our M-79 gunner to hit the small rooftop. The hotel was tall but it was unusually small. It looked out of proportion to me, almost like a column. I didn't want to waste any M-79 rounds. We were going to need all we had before the day was over.

We made it about 50 yards further and began to get pinned down by small-arms fire. When I could hear the sound of B-40's exploding, I knew it was time to "waste" a few rounds. Phat and the guys were anxious to start firing. As soon as I got "Buy muy chin" (seventy-nine) out of my mouth, our man started firing at the top of the hotel. If I didn't know any better, I'd say he must have been bore-sighting his weapon while he was waiting for the OK to fire. The first round dropped neatly on top of the small roof. The two VC on the roof disappeared in the smoke and debris from the explosion.

Not waiting for the word or any discussion, we all charged forward toward the building that was directly opposite the hotel. When we stopped, we were met by a hail of gunfire from the ground floor of the hotel. The M-79 gunner dropped a round in the front door and silenced them. I motioned that we were to assault the building.

I rushed across the street, stopped just below a first-floor window and tossed a grenade through the opening. After it went off, four of the PRUs went in the front room. The first two inside the door were firing as they went through. We hadn't received any more fire from the hotel after the grenade went off. I motioned for some of the others to come in and we started up the stairs.

I have to admit it was a bit spooky working our way up the five floors, particularly not being able to understand what was being said. I let the PRUs go first because they knew the layout and could communicate with the occupants. They also would be able to recognize any fugitive we had on our "black list" who we had been looking for. No doubt, all available VC were committed to this campaign. If they were successful, other provisional government personnel, such as Sau Be, would be in the area as well.

The hotel was the local hangout for the prostitutes and therefore a favorite hangout for my guys as well. We went into each room to make sure we weren't bypassing any bad guys on the way up. Surprisingly the rooms were almost all occupied by either the prostitutes or the visitors to the city for Tet. A few of the rooms were occupied by GVN soldiers who were unarmed. The VC had moved in so fast, they hadn't had time to clear all of the rooms. They also knew the GVN wouldn't pose much of a problem since they weren't armed or organized.

The narrow stairs and the very small rooms made the going extremely close. At best, only two or three guys could move at a time. Often we were bumping into each other. Situations like this were why we preferred to use the Swedish-K sub-machine gun or the small M-2 U.S. carbine. They were perfect to move onto a target with quick, short bursts. Hand grenades were strictly out of the question for us. It was simply too close quarters to use them. The enemy, on the other hand, could drop them down the stairwell without risk to their own.

As we worked our way up, the PRU seemed to get bogged down with the status of the GVN soldiers we were picking up. My troops were pissed off that the GVN weren't out with them fighting the VC. "Let's go, God damn it! We go," and pointed up toward the roof. I understood their problem. I had convinced them that we shouldn't by-pass any VC and in their minds these soldiers could very well be VC too. In the darkness of the hotel, it would be easy for anyone to hide a weapon under a bed or just lay it down.

It was extremely dark since the city power plant had been knocked out in the first hours of the attack and there were few windows in the rooms and practically none in the hallways. Each time we kicked open a door there was screaming by the occupants who thought they surely were going to die. They pleaded for their lives and wouldn't be quiet until we left to go on to the next room. The high-pitched whine of the women actually bothered me more than the explosions of the grenades or the report of the weapons as my men fired as they made their way up the stairs.

Two GVN soldiers were being dragged with the PRUs. The PRUs were actually kicking them to move faster. I hadn't determined whether they were suspects or they were just trying to get the GVNs into the fight. We were picking up discarded weapons and had six AK-47s so far.

"Give the AK to the soldiers," I yelled to the guys in the back and gestured my orders as I always did. This time I had to do more to be understood over the intense noise rather than because of my lack of the Vietnamese language. The PRUs gave them weapons immediately, confirming that they weren't suspects. Both men took their new weapons and moved forward without any further prodding.

We made it to the roof to find two dead VC and one badly wounded who was drawing his last breaths. From the top of the hotel we had a "VC-eye" view of the entire downtown. I couldn't make out the Embassy House but could damn well see where it should be.

We need to hold this place, I thought. If we don't, we'll be coming back here again. More importantly, we will be on the receiving end of their mortars another night. I called the Embassy House and briefed Jim on our progress.

"Ringo, this is Westhaven, over."

"Roger, Westhaven, go ahead."

"We are on the roof of the hotel and have a great view of the city."

"Good work," Jim said. "Do you have any casualties?"

"Two minor ones who will be able to make it back with us."

"Roger, keep us informed."

"Roger, out."

I decided to leave the two GVN soldiers here. We should be able to find some company for them before we departed. We had four more weapons that we could give to them. Phat looked at me for instructions and I explained to him what I'd just decided. He hesitated and seemed to argue a bit, which was uncharacteristic of him. I responded a bit forceful; and he backed off, but it dawned on me that he was concerned about releasing the weapons.

It wasn't because he didn't trust the Vietnamese soldiers with them but because they were his weapons and were worth money to him. We paid a pretty good sum for automatic weapons like the AK-47's we had here. I had to laugh at the thought. They were kind of right. After all, they would be fighting this war forever or most likely until they were killed. Therefore they had to make the most out of it. They didn't have a lot of faith in the Government of Vietnam military leaders and if they lost the war, they would more than likely be killed by the Viet Cong for being so effective.

I picked up one of the AK's and said "beaucoup piaster," acknowledging that I was aware of the bounty. He smiled as did the rest of my troops. This was one hell of a way to fight a war but it was the way to do it here. We could eliminate a lot of weapons and VC infrastructure for much less than the United States was pouring into the effort so far. The dollar amount of our project had to be virtually negligible in the scheme of things. Getting that bit of politics out of the way, we moved down the stairs.

When we captured the hotel, the VC activity in that neighborhood fell off dramatically. I moved down onto the street and into the daylight and I looked off to the west. There I could see a disturbing sight a few blocks away. I moved to take a close look. Phat grabbed my arm and said, "No can do," meaning we shouldn't go there yet.

"OK, OK," and I pulled his arm away and moved along the street to get a better look. He sent three men to accompany me. We trotted on the south side of the street for about 50 meters and I could then make out the burned hulk of a Jeep. It had to be the one Sergeant Williams was in when he was hit. On the back was the mount for the .50-caliber that I had loaned him. I didn't need to get any closer to determine that there had been no survivors and the bodies had been removed. I turned and headed back toward the hotel where Phat and his men were waiting for us.

The PRUs had rounded up three more Vietnamese soldiers and armed them with the remaining VC weapons. I was sure that as soon as we left, a few more friendlies would come out and reinforce the five we had armed. Our group didn't waste any time getting back to the theater and took advantage of the lull we had caused by taking the key lookout on the hotel.

The situation in the city now was that as soon as we took one key VC strongpoint, they would move to another and abandon the old one. That was starting to work to our advantage. We continued to have the momentum and the VC had lost theirs.

Back in front of the theater we were receiving small-arms fire from the same VC that had fired on us when we left the police station for the theater almost an hour before. We couldn't stay there much longer because the front of the theater didn't provide much cover. I pointed to the left side of the theater. The small buildings would provide some cover from the enemy who were firing on us from the taller buildings across the street.

As soon as we went around the corner we found cover among the smaller residential buildings near where we picked up Sau Be. The layout of the houses gave us more cover; and, because they were much closer together, we could move without being seen from the taller buildings to our rear. This area also would give us cover and concealment for about 200 meters as it paralleled the road that led to Major Phoung's house.

The PRUs and I were familiar with operating in the small hamlets and easily maneuvered from house to house, making sure we weren't by-passing any VC. We damned sure didn't want to get ourselves boxed in like they did in the Piney Woods massacre in Wyoming during the Indian Wars. This was the second time I recalled that incident. It no doubt made an impression on me. I thought how I would like to thank the author of that book I had read back at Fort Bragg a few months ago for making that point so clear to me. It kept me from falling into a trap on several occasions in this battle alone.

Clearing these little houses was not as easy as you might think. If you didn't know any better, you would think that these were all VC hooches because they each had what appeared to be a fighting position with an overhead cover dug into the dirt floor in the main room. What they actually were was shelters prepared by the people long ago to protect themselves from the frequent mortar or rocket attack by either the VC or GVN forces.

My troops were doing a great job clearing the hooches without using extreme force, considering we were getting fired on whenever we got too close to the wide street we were paralleling. This street was the one that led to Major Phoung's house and was where I thought the remaining VC command element was positioned. The closer we got to his place, the stronger the enemy resistance appeared to be from the street.

The troops would kick open a door and order the occupants to come out to be identified. Most wouldn't move but remained in their underground hiding places rather than risk being hit by a stray round. I really couldn't blame them because the firing was fairly steady. I guess they figured they'd take their chances with the PRU. The usual method used by the VC and the ARVN to clear a structure was to fire into the building first or simply toss a hand grenade in before they entered. It was the safest way by far but was hard on the civilian population.

I was glad that my guys were under control. They systematically cleared each house. They used our normal technique of one guy at the door, one on each front corner of the building and one backing up the doorman. The doorman would kick open the door and rush in moving to one side. His back-up would rush in and go to the other side. This was a little easier to accomplish here than it would be if it were in the United States because each of the hooches was practically identical. The assault group knew before going in what the general layout was.

We had broken down into four-man teams. I was pleased with the way they were systematically moving through the area. I was positioned with two others providing security from the rear. The rear element seemed to be getting most of the sniper fire because it seemed that the VC had closed in behind us when we left the main street.

I was watching this little drama unfold when one of the guys with my element was hit in the shoulder by fragmentation from a rocket or grenade. His buddy right next to him immediately rushed over to help. Seeing that he wasn't too bad, I continued to fire single shot at the likely sniper positions. The two with me sought cover in a house that had just been cleared. That seemed as good an idea as any because there was no chance to get a medivac and we didn't have a place to take him anyway. Our rear area was the police station and we were cut off from it right then. They motioned for me to go on and quickly closed the door behind them.

I ran up to where Phat was and told him about his two guys. Now we were essentially down to 13, including me. We only had a few meters to go and we would be out of the residential area and had to move back toward the road where we were receiving the most fire. Phat motioned to the last few houses and I gestured for him to clear them and then pointed to the main street where we could barely make out Major Phoung's house. He understood and ordered his men to clear the last hooches.

The PRUs, upon entering the first of the remaining four hooches, recognized a VC who was on our list. We had been looking for him for several weeks. He was a suspected VC village chief who had been captured previously. Somehow he had managed to get away from the PIC. Upon seeing the PRU, he ran out the back of the house. Two PRU were on his tail yelling for him to stop. When he didn't, they shot him. Phat turned to me and smiled and darted over to the body. He quickly searched him and returned with some papers. None of us had time to read them so we proceeded to clear the last building.

We hadn't found any VC, other than the one the PRUs had just killed, but it was obvious that every one of the houses we went into had been occupied by the enemy at one time or another during the offensive. Many had spent copper-colored AK-47 casings scattered on the floor and left-overs from hastily cooked meals. Behind one cluster of hooches was the remnants of an 82mm mortar pit used by the VC during the early phase of the offensive.

We gathered our force together behind the last two buildings to figure out how we were going to move against Major Phoung's house. Phat put out security to cover us while we talked it over. So far we had done OK just taking advantage of the situation and moving fast. We felt this time would be the last big push to get the enemy out of town and if the VC were in numbers, we would have our hands full. I wished we had the .50-caliber with us and wondered how we could get the word to the guys back at the police station.

We still hadn't received much help from the ARVNs to this point and weren't expecting any when one of the PRUs signaled with a hushed whistle to get our attention. Both Phat and I looked up to see a small group of ARVN soldiers, about 20 to 25 of them, trying to move up the street behind us toward Major Phoung's house. They were about 150 meters to our rear and dodging between buildings and trees that dotted the street. I could hear the high pitched shouts of their leaders directing their advance.

The VC had them pinned down pretty good. It looked like the VC were trying to move to positions on top of the tall buildings just to the rear of the friendly positions. If they did, they would be able to inflict heavy casualties on the GVN force. Damn! I wished I had the .50 with us or even the 57-recoilless that we had to leave because both were so cumbersome. From here they could make short work of the VC running around the tops of the buildings fully exposed. That not being the case, we needed to do something fast.

"Phat," I said, and pointed to the edge of the street behind us. There was a short wall on our side, about 50 yards behind us. If we could get back to it, we could provide covering fire for the ARVN unit that was pinned down. So far it didn't look like they had suffered any casualties. We needed to break up the VC attack before there were any casualties. The ARVN platoon might lose interest real fast if they started getting the shit kicked out of them.

Phat understood what was on my mind and relayed my plan to the troops. I was glad we had taken the time to clear the buildings to our rear. I felt we could move back fairly quickly. I took off for the wall with the entire group of PRUs behind me. There was a small pond between us and that wall and I really didn't want to wade through it because, like most pools of water in the villages and even in the city, they were used for sewage. They never really smelled that bad though and I never knew why. Right now that didn't matter. The pond was coming closer and I was committed to it. The PRUs were behind me then and started to hesitate as I waded in.

They followed right behind when the VC on the rooftops saw us and started to take us under fire. A few rounds hit the water just to our right and we pushed ourselves as fast as we could. My weapon was raised up over my head and the water was close to my chin. Only a few feet more and I'd be through. Please don't let me find a hole, I thought. Without looking back, I knew the PRU were in trouble. After all, I was a good six inches taller than the tallest one.

I started to come out of the water about 20 feet from the wall. I could see the VC moving on the rooftops trying to figure out which element to engage. We had them confused, which was a good sign. The GVN unit hadn't seen us yet but knew something was up. They also knew we were in the area because I was sure they were trying to either help us or join up with us for their own protection. Whatever the reason, we were helping each other and confusing the hell out of the enemy.

The VC commander must be trying to figure out how far to take this campaign. Right now it had to be looking futile to him. Any good commander has to calculate his losses against the value of the objective. Sure Chau Phu city, if they could hold it, would be a prize. I hated the concept of body count but as a leader in the field, I still needed to try to figure out what the enemy strength was.

I mentally began a calculation of VC losses to date. I knew they had lost more than 40 KIA as a direct result of the PRUs and myself. I was sure we killed at least 10 or 12 with the SEALs before Ted was hit. They must have lost a few to the isolated pockets of ARVN soldiers cut off during the attack. I saw two VC in the CORDs compound who probably were killed by Dennis and Arturo. That matched up with what they told me after I pulled them out of there.

I was sure the PBRs accounted for 30 or so killed at the hospital. I saw several dead VC in front of the hospital before they gave that place up as a bad idea. Then of course we had 20 POWs. I was sure that the police lieutenant and his little unit accounted for at least six who I saw lying on the ground in front of their position. I doubted that the TOC defenders had killed any but I couldn't be sure.

Up until now I suspected that the 510th VC battalion had

attacked the city. That battalion was thought to have a field strength of about 300. Let's see now. I made a quick calculation as I waited for the rest of my troops to reach me. In the 15 or 20 seconds it took for them to make it across the "People's Pool," I counted 88 enemy KIA. To account for my error and the possibility of counting bodies twice, I cut that in half. That makes 44. Then of course there were the 20 POWs who we actually had our hands on. That makes the enemy losses at 64 not counting their wounded who are out of action. That's a good slice out of any unit. Coupled with the loss of a key leader, that put their situation a bit tenuous.

The last PRU, who was Phat, made it out of the water and positioned himself next to me. "Mr. Trew?" he asked, looking for direction.

"VC!" I pointed to the roofline where two or three could be seen. He started to direct his men to fire on them but I grabbed his arm to stop him. The VC had stopped firing on the ARVN platoon. I wanted to watch for a minute to see who would make the next move.

Meanwhile the ARVN platoon pulled off the road and found better cover in some trees within a small courtyard that surrounded a large building of some sort. Good, I thought, they are out of the woods for the time being. Now let's see what the VC are up to. If I didn't know any better, I'd bet they were considering how to get out of this mess they're in. They probably won't make their move until dark. They don't want to risk being caught in the open if we ever get any air support.

If they knew what I knew, they would leave now. There was no hope of any air support anytime soon. At least not any U.S. air support. I couldn't be sure what Major Phoung was arranging. I was sure he would be screaming for it and some would eventually show up and start bombing the shit out of the place regardless of where the friendlies were.

What we were up against now, I was pretty sure, was pockets of resistance that couldn't get out or link up with other elements. This was good and bad. We probably would have to tangle with VC who didn't want any more to do with us. Ordinarily we would jump at the chance to go after them, but we were still vastly outnumbered and I was still guessing on whether only one VC battalion was committed in the fight.

We had about 100 meters to go before we got to Major Phoung's house. The only way to it was along the wide street that ran directly from where we were. We were only about 10 meters from the road. Phat and I both knew what that meant. As soon as we exposed ourselves we would catch shit from all directions except from where the ARVN platoon was located about 70 meters directly across the street from us. We needed to move now while that platoon was there to help us.

We decided to split into two elements. One element of five men would cross the street at our location and set up next to a building that would give them clear fields of fire in both directions on the street. They would have the M-60. It looked like they would be OK if they made it across. The rest of us would stay on our side and move to the end of the street, where Major Phoung's house was.

The greatest immediate risk to this was to the five who were going to dash across the street. I didn't want to lose any of them, but I really was worried about losing the M-60. If they made it across, we probably would be able to tell where most of the enemy positions were when they opened up on our small group. Of course we would be able to provide a substantial amount of effective supporting fire from the security of the three-foot-high wall we were behind now.

Then it would be our turn. From what we could see, there wasn't much cover from our present position all the way to the major's house. The only protection was a curb that was little more than 10 inches high that ran between the street and the sidewalk. We couldn't maneuver further to the right because that was an open corridor more than a hundred feet wide that ran the entire distance to the house. The open area was more like a field with several water obstacles. So far, no enemy activity had been seen in that direction. Of course there were no guarantees there weren't any there.

I looked at all of the men and wondered what was actually going on in their minds as we continued to push ourselves. All eyes were on the first five as they readied themselves and secured their equipment for the 30-meter dash to the other side. The others peeled off the 75- to 100-round belts of linked 7.62 ammo for the M-60 they had been carrying. The guys going across the street were the only ones who would need it.

The firing had almost dropped off completely in the city with the exception of the sporadic popping sounds of snipers from either side taking pot shots at targets of opportunity. This sudden drop of small-arms fire added to the anticipation of the moment. We knew that, despite all the wishful thinking, the VC hadn't just vanished. They were still there and just as determined as ever to kill us as we were to kill them.

The five decided to all move at once. To move one or two at a time in some interval was asking for trouble in the city where the enemy could be anywhere and the real estate was completely flat and all of the cover and concealment spots were so predictable. The enemy could anticipate where you were likely to be running to and where you would most likely appear again.

All five took deep breaths and lunged for the other side of the street. They were halfway there before the enemy opened up on them. It sounded like a mad minute from an infantry platoon. As soon as the enemy opened up, we fired everything we could on full automatic. The ARVN platoon also began firing in the direction of the enemy on the rooftops. The volume of fire from our side gradu-ally picked up intensity as the enemy started to split up and maneuver. They were less than 100 meters from us and well concealed.

It was difficult to pick out specific targets. In fact, I tried but couldn't make out any at all. Then I could see the blunt end of a rocket protrude from a window. Everyone seemed to see him at the same time because all our fire seemed to swing over toward him. He managed to get his B-40 off but it went wild past us and struck the pavement close to Major Phoung's house. Another rocket managed to hit a tree just over the heads of the five PRUs across the street.

After the smoke settled, I could tell that at least two of the PRUs were hit because the others were looking after them. Their attention was soon diverted back to the enemy as the small-arms fire picked up again. This time VC who were at the other end of the street near Major Phoung's house joined in the fire fight. The injured PRU must not have been too bad because they immediately began returning fire.

"Let's go, Phat," I yelled. The 8 of us jumped up and started running toward the major's house. We fired as we ran, and the enemy firing from that direction ducked back into the buildings.

The M-79 man began dropping rounds on top of the building to our rear and that seemed to be effective in keeping their heads down. Their volume of fire was still significant, but became very wild and not very close to our positions at all. Our M-79 man had found a good position behind a wall that allowed him to take careful aim. The VC had to keep their heads down or risk getting them blown off.

We were now half-way to our objective and were only receiving pot shots as we made our way closer to Major Phoung's house. I started to feel a little more comfortable and just then all hell broke loose on us from the house. We kept running toward it because there wasn't any place to hide. The enemy concentrated their fire on me and I dropped to the ground and found that I could get behind that 10- to 12-inch curb. Phat and the others found their own little piece of curb and we began a shoot-out from there. I happened to be in the front of the column when we got hit hard.

We must have made pretty small targets, all pasted to that tiny wall. We inched our way along the wall but the VC kept up a steady assault on us. There appeared to be at least a squad of infantry firing full automatic at us. Our M-60 was busy with the VC behind us and that element couldn't help any more than they already were. Actually they were helping a lot because if they weren't there, the VC would be coming down the street after us. While I was contemplating my next move, I could hear our 57-recoilless rifle firing to our rear. There were now three elements of friendlies in the immediate area. The ARVN platoon, my troops at the police station and us. All were heavily engaged at the moment and that was taking the heat off of each other. That's just the kind of help we needed right then.

I was crouched so low that I couldn't aim my Swedish-K at all. To do so would require that I raise up a few inches and I damn well couldn't afford to do that. I laid the barrel on its side and fired with the bolt handle facing up. The enemy rounds were hitting so close that I was afraid that debris, kicked up from them, would foul the chamber on my weapon as it worked back and forth. We couldn't stay here, I thought. If we didn't get wiped out soon, we'd certainly run out of ammo and get finished off anyway. It was now or never.

"Let's go," I yelled for all of the group to hear. Without hesitation, all of the PRUs jumped up and followed me. We rushed to the next bit of cover, which was a two-foot high wall around a small cemetery. It still was not much cover for the amount of fire we were receiving but it was one hell of a lot better than the place we just left. I had read once and heard it said a hundred times "war is hell;" but how can anything be so bad when a person learns to appreciate little things in life. Right now we all felt really good about having that low wall between us and the enemy.

From my new position, I had a clear view of the front of Major Phoung's house. At least two VC were firing at us from the windows of the second floor. On the ground level, the VC had a machine-gun position just behind the left corner of the wall that encircled the house. That gun was going to pose the biggest threat to our advance. We had to cover at least 50 meters of open area from our present position to the front door.

The street was very wide right there and in front of the walled compound was an island of some sort that had a flagpole in the middle. Instead of the usual yellow and red Vietnamese national flag that flew there, the gold star of the Viet Cong flag was at the top of the staff.

The PRUs behind me were really pouring out the fire from the relative security of the wall. At least they seemed to be getting the advantage over the VC firing from the building. To my rear, I could hear the light "thunk" of a mortar round being dropped into a tube. From the sound I judged the tube to be not more than a couple hundred meters away. Obviously they still have a mortar in town and are willing to bring it in on their own position to break up our attack. We had to move now because I was sure the VC calling in the fire was doing it from the upstairs of the house.

I started getting myself together to get up and lead an advance across the street. Just then one lone VC ran out of the front of Major Phoung's house. He ran in a straight line directly toward us but stopped at the base of the flagpole in the open. We all hesitated for an instant seeing this bizarre behavior. He looked right at us and took up a defiant stance as if to dare us to take down his flag. I looked back at my troops to see if they were seeing what I had seen. They had and I turned and took him up on his dare and finished him with a long burst from my Swedish-K.

Before I fired, I almost wished there had been a better way out for him. He was either very brave or very stupid. I'd like to think it was the former; and I have thought about that guy many times since. I wonder what was going on in his mind. He knew he was going to die. If not from us, from their own mortars that were dropping all around him in the street.

The rounds were beginning to get a little more concentrated and soon they would be on us. They were getting some real effective forward observer support, I thought. I was sure it was from the house we were headed for. Now was the time to move. The enemy small-arms fire, including their machine gun, had dropped to almost nothing as they hunkered down for protection from their own mortar fire. Right now we had to worry about that as well. Now that we were in the same boat, it was the time to move out.

The rest of my group knew it too and they, to the last man, acknowledged they were ready. I raised up and ran directly toward the house, stopping momentarily at the base of the flagpole. I pulled out my knife and cut the lanyard and the flag floated down. I untied it and stuffed it into my shirt and continued on toward the opening in the front wall that used to be the gate.

I was surprised how fast my men made it across the street. By the time I hit the opening in the wall, the rest of my troops were to my left strung out along it with me. Looking to the rear, I saw that one of my troops didn't make it across. He lay not far from the VC at the base of the flagpole. No time for him. We had to keep moving while we were on a roll.

The VC who were upstairs either didn't see us dash across the street or the wall now blocked their view of us. Whatever, we liked it. To my left, I could make out the PRU truck traveling toward us at a high rate of speed. That was a good sign. They must have seen us or the VC were out of the picture back there. The situation was beginning to look up. I knew better than to let my guard down. It seems whenever I did, we almost always got bitten.

I peered through the gate and could see directly into the front door of the house. The door had long since been torn off its hinges. There was no sign of the enemy but I could hear someone scampering around upstairs. Just because I didn't see anybody didn't mean they were gone. I ran at full speed toward the front door that was only 15 or 20 feet from my position.

Out of the corner of my eye, and practically in mid-stride, I caught a glimpse of what looked like the body of Major Phoung's bodyguard. His face was gone but in that fleeting moment I could determine that he had been executed by a shot to the back of the head. He surely must have put up a great stand before he was overwhelmed. There were dozens of empty M-79 casings littered around the front entrance and at each corner of the small courtyard. He still wore the flak jacket that was his trademark. Some of us had joked that he must have worn that thing to bed.

I ducked just inside the front door and knelt down while I waited for the PRUs to make it into the compound. I yelled for Phat to come inside, which he did. "Phat," I said, and motioned for him to position some men outside and to watch alongside of the building. He understood and quietly gave his instructions to the men just outside of the door.

He then pointed up the wide stairs as if he wanted to know my intentions. I pointed to the two side rooms that were to our left, indicating that we needed to check them out before we went up. One PRU, upon seeing me gesture toward those down stair rooms, rushed toward the first and tossed a grenade into it before I could stop him. The entire house was immediately engulfed in smoke from the concussion and plaster fell from the ceiling all over us.

I grabbed Phat by the arm and said, "Thieu Ta Phoung Ba" and shrugged my shoulders as if I wondered where Major Phoung's wife was. It probably hadn't occurred to my troops that his wife could be in there. If it had, they didn't really seem to care. To the contrary, my main reason for coming here now was that if we found them alive maybe the major would show a little more interest in the defense of the city.

I said, "No hai muoi sow," meaning M-26 (grenade). He understood and chastised his men to take care. That was scary, I thought. We just told the VC, if there were any still inside the house, we weren't going to use grenades.

As I started up the stairs, we received automatic-weapons fire from a room at the head of the stairs and also from the second room to our left front downstairs. The three of us who were inside traded shots with them and we started inching our way up. Two other PRUs came into the house following Phat's orders and pursued the VC on the ground floor.

The volume of fire was deafening and the shouts of the VC and my men were barely audible. The situation was chaotic but we were still under control. I got to the top of the stairs and covered Phat and the other man as they came up. The three of us rushed the room at the same time and almost collided as we reached the doorway. I got there first and saw two VC, one of them badly wounded, vault through the open window, firing over their shoulders. The windowsill was covered with a heavy streak of dark blood from where the wounded man drug himself over.

I lunged toward the window and expected to see them crumpled on the ground two stories below. There was no sign of either of them but a blood trail was clearly visible from just below the window to a point where it disappeared behind a building more than 20 meters away.

I could hear the two men who went into the room with me calling out with a great deal of excitement. In the corner of the room behind me, they were yelling for someone to come out from behind some debris. From the tone of their voice, they weren't about to wait very much longer for a response. Just before they were going to hose the place down, a woman and two children emerged. I couldn't make out exactly what my guys were saying, but it appeared that this was Major Phoung's wife and children. They were badly shaken but other than that OK. The woman was overjoyed with the rescue of her children. Through her tears she begged to know how her husband was. Upon hearing that he was alive, she was overwhelmed.

"OK, we must go now. Phat," I said, "Di di mau. VC come." I gestured for all of us to go. We couldn't get caught up here. The mortar fire had stopped for now. Probably because their forward observer was out of action. We had to go, this area was still full of bad guys.

The PRU truck had pulled up in front and I could hear the chatter of the troops going over the latest action of the last few minutes. To emphasize my point to get out of here, I ran to the bottom of the steps and herded the group ahead of me. I told Phat to take the Major's wife to the TOC or turn them over to the Vietnamese we had seen earlier. Standing in the front yard, I could make out the ARVN platoon moving toward us.

"Leave 10 men here so VC no come back." I said. Phat seemed to understand my pigeon Vietnamese almost immediately. We were beginning to communicate better than we had ever done before, but then we probably hadn't spoken as many words over the past three months as we had today.

I planned to ride the truck as far as the Police Headquarters to get my Jeep. I'd follow him to the TOC. I wanted to get an update on the friendly situation and run a few things by Jim. Before we left, I called the Embassy House on the PRC-25.

"Ringo, Westhaven, over."

"Go ahead," was the almost immediate response from Ringo.

"We have Major Phoung's wife and children. They are OK."

"Roger. What are your plans, over?"

"We plan to go to the TOC and see what is going on there."

"Roger, Westhaven. I'll meet you there if I can get out."

"Roger. We'll be there in one-zero, out."

Mrs. Phoung and her two small children climbed into the front seat of the pick-up. Six men and I jumped into the bed of the truck along with the man with our M-60. They didn't waste any time moving out. I could see that our M-60 gunner was out of ammo except for about 50 rounds wrapped around the gun's receiver group. I figured he must have fired over 2,000 rounds. None of the men had any linked belts left. We were getting pretty light so it was about time to re-supply ourselves.

It only took a few minutes to get back to the police station from Major Phoung's house. We passed the ARVN platoon about half way there. It looked like they were headed toward the Major's house and from what I could see, they were in pretty good spirits considering there were fewer than 20 men in the platoon. That would be plenty to hold the house it the VC tried to take it back. That is if we were still pressing them from their rear.

The pick-up pulled up to the front gate and I hopped out of the back. I motioned for one of the PRU to come with me and he gladly followed me into the police compound. I needed someone to hold the .50-caliber while I drove. The two of us climbed on board the Jeep and we raced to catch up with the pick-up. The ride back to the TOC was fairly quiet but a little spooky considering the two of us were on our own. The pick-up wasn't wasting any time getting through the bad part of town and had long since left us. The "automatic gates" opened for us as we approached.

Major Phoung was standing by the PRU pick-up embracing his wife. Both children were holding on to his legs, not wanting to let go. Jim walked up to me and as usual was all business.

"What does it look like downtown, Drew?"

"Well, Jim, it looks like the VC are trying to get their act together so they can get the hell out of town. How is it going at the Embassy House?"

"We haven't had much activity for the past few hours. I think you're right, it looks like they have given up the attack on Chau Doc. Yeah, Drew, things are definitely looking up. Major Phoung here seems to be getting his act together."

It sure didn't take him long to get back to his old self. Major Phoung had just said good-bye to his wife and children and turned away, barking orders to his troops.

"Drew," Jim said, "an ARVN unit is coming up the road this afternoon sometime. I think it may be a Ranger unit and they'll come in from the south from Can Tho."

"I take it from that, the situation in Can Tho is under control."

"Yeah, Drew, it's getting better fast. In fact it seems that the VC are being contained all over the country. They really hit hard in Saigon and in I CORPS, especially Hue City and they are really dug in up there. The Marines are having a hell of a time up there trying to root them out. However from what I can make out, they have it under control. The Marines are really taking some casualties in the street fighting up there. You probably know what it must be like from the situation we have here. Tell me about it." "We've had a bit of luck on our side but it can be nasty!"

# CHAPTER 11

## BREAKING THROUGH!

"Where are the SEALs, Jim?"

"They are coming in off the river and should be at the house by this evening. Too bad they were pulled off, Drew."

"Yeah but it worked out anyway. What about Risher?"

"It's confirmed. He didn't make it. He was pretty bad. I told you before that Maggie didn't think he had much of a chance. She and Scollice had a problem keeping his airway open. They even used a piece of engine hose or something like that to suck out the fluid in his throat. I guess they really worked on him until he was medivaced."

"Too bad," I said. "He did a good job on the run in to get the civilians and later on the roof. He didn't hesitate to climb up there."

It's common when someone is killed to reflect on the circumstances surrounding a situation as soon as things start to settle down, as they were now.

"What about Maggie, Jim?"

"She made it back a few hours ago. She went with the civilians to Long Xuyen. They stayed there a few hours and then on to Can Tho. Somehow she managed to stay onboard until just a few hours ago. Then I got this radio call from the skipper on the LCM. He said he had this woman on board who wanted off at the Embassy House. He said she threatened to jump overboard and swim if he didn't put her ashore.

"I told him to bring her in. I guess he didn't think we had the place secure because he started to prep the landing area. I had to shut him off before he destroyed the place."

"Jim, I thought they would ship all of the volunteers, like Maggie, back stateside."

"They are, but she apparently has other ideas," he replied.

"Drew, we're getting low on ammunition. I've requested a re-supply of an assortment of small-arms ammo and grenades."

"That's a good idea. The PRUs are going through the grenades like they're sowing seed."

"I thought so."

"How are they going to bring it in?" I asked.

"Our people are going to air drop it on the airfield by a Caribou. They should be on their way any time now. The PRUs will know what's up when they see the aircraft come in. This way we don't have to run the drop. We can get the supplies anytime we need.

"Drew, Bao and some men have been in and out of the city several times since you were at Major Phoung's house. By the way, Drew, that was a good move getting his wife and children out. Major Phoung is a changed man."

"Yeah, I noticed."

"Drew, he's acting like it never happened. He may never get over the loss of respect he suffered by acting so distressed."

"I know, Jim, I hope we can work with him in the future. He's been good to work with—not at all like the province chief." "We've always been able to get things done through him when the province chief wanted payment to use our own military equipment we've given them. It's the craziest thing I've ever seen but I doubt if it will change now. The whole situation is the shits. We're winning the ground war about every place you look and the outcome of the war is not that clear."

"Yeah, Drew, we're on a roll down here in the province and have things going our way most of the time. Charlie gave us his best shot and I think we have him on the run."

Jim had a great philosophy about things. He made it a point to avoid the politics of most situations and therefore wasn't affected by political pressure from Saigon. We both respected the enemy as a worthy adversary; after all they were Vietnamese too. The main difference was their leadership. We just did what needed to be done.

I couldn't argue with Jim's philosophy. It worked for him and kept him alive, despite having his ass hung out in these remote assignments with only the support he arranged for himself. He was young, just like me, but I was learning a lot from him and hoped that it would keep me alive in the future.

There were two types of people in the business we were in. There were those like Jim Moore and our boss in Can Tho, Jim Ward, who had enough confidence in themselves to let their subordinates loose to do their own thing. Then there were the others who felt the urge to over-supervise. They were the ones who were afraid to get involved with any unpopular decision. They were so afraid to make a decision that you literally flounder in the field for lack of guidance. They were the ones that got guys killed!

Before I left the PRUs, I told them to go to their camp and report to Bao. I spoke to each of them, thanking them for a job well done. I made a special effort to impress on Phat that I thought he was a real combat leader and I would tell Bao that he did a great job. This probably had the most impact on him as he was extremely loyal to Bao and respected him over life itself.

We left the Vietnamese to their business and loaded our vehicles and headed for the Embassy House. The short trip was getting extremely routine but now the enemy wasn't posing any real threat when we passed the hospital. Jim rode with me in my Jeep with Nago on the .50-caliber. The two other Nungs who accompanied Jim to the TOC followed in the second Jeep.

The street in front of the Embassy House was still deserted. The people living in the little houses must be getting pretty ripe. They hadn't been out of their homes since the offensive started just over 40 hours ago.

The Jeeps pulled up to the double gates and two Nungs, one on each gate, pulled them open. All of the Nungs, with the exception of the one on the roof and the ones positioned on the river, greeted us with smiles and excited chatter. Normally reserved, they were obviously happy that I had made it back from downtown in one piece.

After a few minutes of small talk with the Nungs, I went into my room and dropped off some of my gear. From my room, I could hear what sounded like an aircraft overhead. I went out into the courtyard where I could get a better look. It looked like the Air America Caribou that Jim said would be dropping badly needed ammunition. All of the units in the city were also in short supply. The Vietnamese at the TOC and the Special Forces B-Team, at the other end of town, were in the worst shape.

Jim had tried to get the Vietnamese and the U.S. military, through the B-Team, to re-supply us, since we were the only ones really putting up a fight. Lt. Col. Smith, the B-Team commander, had told

Jim that Chau Doc was on its own because of the over-all situation in the country. It seems that Chau Doc had a pretty low priority because major headquarters elements were being hit and no air support was available for us until that situation stabilized.

Jim arranged an air-drop through our channels. As usual, the Air America crews were willing to give it a try and they obviously had made it this far. Westy was on the roof talking with them on the HT-2 air-to-ground radio.

"Roger," he said. "Line up over the confluence of the two rivers and pick up a heading toward the proposed airfield."

"Roger," was the pilot's response. "I see the field and what looks like the camp out in the open."

"That's it," Westy replied as the Caribou banked hard to the left just over the B-Team compound. The aircraft was less than 700 feet up and coming in fast.

Jim and I hurried up to the roof to get a better view of the drop. The plane would pass directly to our front as it headed to the PRU camp. I could hear the pilot call that he was taking small-arms fire from the city. Westy didn't answer but watched as we all held our breath. The aircraft was very vulnerable as it seemed to hang there in front of us.

The tail gate was already open and as soon as the aircraft reached the camp, it dropped its load. Three parachutes popped neatly out the back and the Caribou strained to gain altitude. It looked like Bao wouldn't have to go very far to recover that load. From our position, it was right on target. The two of us started back off the roof, leaving Westy to finish talking with the pilot.

I looked around and could see considerable evidence that the folks at the Embassy House had been pretty busy too. There were spent casings and used hand-held flare canisters strewn all over the ground.

The .50-caliber was there, still secured in the 55-gallon drum. Because the gun shook the roof so much, we welded a heavy piece of flat steel to the bottom of the pedestal and put that inside the drum. We then filled the drum with sandbags to keep the gun from vibrating too much. Even so, after we fired the gun any length of time, Westy's room was covered with plaster- and concrete-dust that had fallen from the ceiling. That was a hell of a lot better than the first time we tried the gun from there. The gun actually rattled chunks of concrete from the ceiling and a huge crack developed on the side of the building. We thought we would have to abandon the idea of having the gun up there until we came up with the idea of the drum.

Jim and I were in the back office getting ready to get on the single sideband to give a situation report when Westy came running in.

"Jim, Drew, it looks like they were right on target but I think the kicker took a round through the jaw. At least that's what it sounded like from the pilot. We'll check on that when we get normal communications back. We can't do anything about that now."

"They sure came through for us," I said.

"Yeah, they always find a way don't they," Jim added.

Westy chimed in that he talked with the Navy boats which had been cruising the river. "The SEALs are on their way in and should be here any time now."

Jim responded, "I think we should set up a defense here and wait for the ARVNs to come in from the south. We don't need to get in a cross-fire with some trigger-happy troops."

"I agree," I told them. "Most of the town is secure except for isolated pockets, and they will try to make a run for it when it gets dark soon."

"Drew, do you think we can make it to the B-Team?"

"What do you mean, Jim?"

"I mean you and I need to go over there and see what is going on."

"Good idea and we can get some beer. We're a little short if the SEALs get back."

Jim was an adventurous sort. I knew that he really wanted to see what condition our town was in and he couldn't wait any longer. "That sounds great," he said. "Let's go then. Come on Nago, you go too." He smiled about getting a reprieve from having to stay at the Embassy House any longer.

I got behind the wheel, Nago took control of the .50-caliber and Jim hopped in the suicide seat. Siew opened the gate on Nago's command. I accelerated to about 40 miles an hour, still anticipating an ambush at the hospital. None came but I didn't slow down much because we were going through a part of the city neither of us had been in since the attack. I had only gotten within three blocks of the B-Team at different times over the past few hours of doing battle with the VC. I didn't want to get in to a cross-fire with them. We had our hands full as it was, and the Special Forces would be able to take care of themselves.

The Special Forces compound was a rather formidable place. It consisted of a walled complex that included a large, solidly built main building which housed the mess hall and the bar. It actually seemed more like a castle than a military complex. To the rear of the main building, within the wall, were several rather plain buildings that served as barracks, warehouses and offices for the U.S. Special Forces. The B-Team supported the A-Team located in the highly disputed Seven Mountains area of the province. Most of the other Special Forces camps had been turned over as part of the Vietnamization program that was underway throughout the country. The Seven Mountains was a hotbed of VC activity and it wasn't practical to turn this particular camp over to the Vietnamese yet.

The B-Team was a great place to go and unwind between operations. We often went there to have a meal with the SF types. They were a good bunch of guys and we had made several good friends there. They had a fine bar; and since Jim and I had immunity from the curfews imposed by the Vietnamese, we could travel throughout the city without interference.

Sometimes when I wasn't in the field, Jim and I would take Maggie to the B-Team to watch a movie. Whenever we did, everyone seemed to look at us with their mouths open. We probably did look a little strange, driving my Jeep in with the .50-caliber on it ready for action.

I guess we stretched the intent of the special status a bit, but in order for us to gain the notoriety we needed to be effective, we acted like we owned the place. This was probably a sore spot with Lt. Col. Smith, but we really didn't care. Soon after Tet, he was replaced by Major Reed. Both Jim and I liked the change and enjoyed the fine working relationship we developed with him.

I pulled the Jeep up to the front gate. At that point we were directly in front of the Chinese noodle factory across the river—the place where the VC often set up rockets or mortars to attack the B-Team. We could see the indigenous guards through the gate. They weren't making any move to open the gate for us. I guess they figured that the town was still under VC control and weren't expecting any visitors. Nago yelled some profanity in the best Vietnamese he could muster and the guard called for one of the American sergeants to come.

The sergeant quickly recognized us and gave the order to open the gate. I pulled in and stopped at the front door to the main building just a few feet inside. Nago stayed with the Jeep and as we walked away we could hear him proudly answering the barrage of questions being fired at him by the Vietnamese guards. We walked into the bar, which was the first room inside the building.

"I guess it's not open," I said to Jim.

"I guess not," he laughed.

Two SF sergeants came up to us and began asking questions about the city and the VC activity. They actually thought we had rescued them and were surprised that we had "broken through."

"No, we really didn't break through," I said. "We just came to get a couple of cases of beer."

They kind of laughed over that and departed as Colonel Smith walked up. He appeared annoyed that we were there. Jim attempted to brief him, but he didn't seem too interested in what Jim had to say.

"Let's go," Jim said and we turned to leave. I saw a couple sergeants whom I had known at Fort Bragg as we went back to the Jeep.

"Drew," one of them said, "thanks for the loan of the 81mm mortar. It came in pretty handy."

"Don't mention it," I replied. "We'll try to get you some more ammo for it."

"Great! We could use more illumination rounds."

"I'll see what I can do."

We both climbed into the Jeep and noticed five cases of beer stacked in the back. One of the sergeants said it was on the house and saluted as we drove out the gate.

"Jim, what do you think about that?"

"What's that, Drew?"

"The guys back there thinking we 'broke through' to get to them."

"Yeah, it's too bad those guys weren't let loose on the city with you and the PRUs. They sure wanted to go but were not allowed to leave."

We both got a good laugh over the beer-run mission.

"You know, Jim, what's really funny about us going to the B-

Team for beer is that you don't drink."

Again, Jim laughed and said, "I guess I could have briefed the colonel if he was interested."

We joked about that the entire way back to the Embassy House. It was the first real laugh we had since the offensive started 43 hours before.

"Maybe the rest of the SEALs will be back when we get there," Jim said, trying to get us back to some sense of seriousness. "They will be ready to get back into the action after being on the river since Risher was hit. We'll probably have to hold them until the ARVNs make their push through the city."

"Yeah, Jim, the ARVNs should be able to clear out the town pretty fast now that we have taken most of the major strongholds."

"We'll see how well they do," Jim replied with obvious skepticism in his voice. "In any case they should be reaching Chau Phu soon."

The Embassy House was just ahead and the lead elements of an ARVN unit were approaching from the south. From what I could see, it looked like at least a battalion of infantry moving on both sides of the road. The column stretched out for more than a mile. Helicopter gunships were circling overhead and were making wide cloverleaf maneuvers, just ahead of the advancing force. Their pattern covered the entire southern limits of the city to the west, and the eastern gunship team extended all the way to the east bank of the Bassac River.

The helicopters worked in pairs. A light observation helicopter flew ahead at tree-top level while the gunships flew at a higher altitude and to the rear a few hundred meters. The idea was for the observation helicopter to draw fire from the ground and the HUIH would answer with its mini-guns and rockets.

The plan seemed to work because the little guinea pig on the west started drawing fire from the area close to where the PRUs and I went through to get to Major Phoung's house. The gunship quickly let loose with it's mini-guns and rockets simultaneously. In no time the other team flying over the river joined in and all hell broke loose. We pulled into the compound and Jim, Nago and I went up to the rooftop to watch the fireworks.

The tables have clearly turned, I thought. The VC were now on the receiving end of overwhelming firepower. The gunships were giving the VC everything they had and this time only a meager string of green tracers shot skyward. The ARVN unit immediately moved off of the road in the direction of the action. They were advancing toward the west and formed on line to attack the tree line and small hooches on the edge of the city. The unit was no longer in view but we could hear the exchange of small-arms fire a few hundred meters away and could follow their progress from the sound.

"Jim, I hope the ARVNs brought a lot of ammo with them," I said.

From the volume of fire, they had already used up a normal basic load. More helicopters joined in and really were letting the VC have it. It would be surprising if there was anything left of that part of town when they got done. In no time, that area of the city was in flames. Large clouds of black smoke began to cover the entire area.

I guess we were all lucky that the Vietnamese Air Force wasn't in the fight. We'd all be in trouble. Their airmen were famous for dropping 250 pounders anywhere they felt like it. Their air-to-ground coordination was never very good; and the animosity between the Vietnamese Army and the Vietnamese Air Force was a known fact.

On a few operations in the past when I had worked with Vietnamese ground units, the ground commanders would call for air strikes. Several hours would pass and no air support. The ground troops would give up waiting; and, as soon as they would try to advance, the Air Force would come, often without making radio contact. They would start dropping their ordinance on the coordinates given in the initial request. Needless to say, the situation usually turned bad in a hurry as 250 pounders started dropping around the friendlies. I often wondered what the VC were thinking when this happened.

I went downstairs during this lull to get some gear ready and try to get a few minutes rest. We all felt that the major threat to the city was over. What we were concerned about was the possible risk of the ARVNs pushing the VC into us. We'd be ready for them though. The Nungs had been cleaning all of our weapons at intervals throughout the battle. They already had gotten a re-supply of ammunition from Bao, which came on the air drop, and they were busy breaking open the crates and disseminating the ammunition to the person responsible for each particular weapon. Without the usual commotion and rapid-fire dialogue that went along with anything they did, each ran off with his load. I was glad that the Nungs still felt the need to be prepared and would be especially watchful during the night.

I was tired but I also knew that everyone else at the Embassy House was in about the same situation. Before I went to crash for a couple hours, I told Maan to relay to Vinh that each of the Nungs should get some sleep before night. Jim and I knew that there would be a lot of commotion tonight with the ARVN unit in town. They'd be firing at anything that moved and the VC definitely would try to make a break for the border during the night.

At least the Embassy House wasn't in their likely escape route. There was no way we would be able to sleep through that. The fighting right now was scarcely 300 to 400 meters to our front. Some of it was just behind the Catholic Church that was directly across the street.

I woke to the sound of men scurrying overhead and the thump of our 60mm mortar firing illumination rounds from the roof. Even with the rubber tires as a cushion, the base plate smacked the roof over my head. I grabbed my Swedish-K and ran up to the roof. Some of the SEALs were there. They obviously had arrived while I was sleeping. I could see their large silhouettes moving around among the smaller one of the Nungs.

"Hey, Drew," one of them said. "About time you got up."

"I felt like I died when I hit the rack," I told the group.

Jim was up there as well and said the VC apparently were making a break for it. All hell broke loose at the west end of town and toward the canal.

"They are trying to get to the border like we thought they would " Jim said.

"Yeah," I replied. "I hope the Air Force chases them all the way to Phnom Penh. There's really no cover for them for at least a couple of miles after they cross over the border."

Aircraft were flying overhead, dropping long-burning parachute flares which lit up the sky for several minutes. We couldn't see the ground from where we were standing but I knew the terrain well enough to know where the action was. It was as flat as a pool table and there wasn't anything higher than a pool ball for them to hide behind.

Jim said, "This is it for them. I doubt if there'll be much work for you guys tomorrow."

No sooner had Jim finished his statement than Khanh, Jim's interpreter who had finally made it to the compound, came running up: "Bao is on the radio and said that some VC are in front of camp, not too far away."

"Maybe we can support him," I yelled and immediately turned the 60mm mortar which was just behind us toward the camp. I used Kentucky windage to direct the gun in the general proximity of the camp. Nago knew what I wanted and had an illumination round ready to drop in the tube.

"OK, Nago, one illumination round."

Nago, in classic mortarman style, knelt down and eased a round into the tube. He dropped below the tube opening to avoid being struck by the round as it left the tube. Nago loved the mortar. We had fired many rounds of the larger 81mm mortar together over the past few months while at one of our remote PRU camps north of An Phu.

The illumination round popped and appeared just over the west end of the PRU compound. Khanh, the interpreter, was on the radio with Bao: "Bao said that the flare is good. Can we use the mortar and fire at the VC? He can see them in the fields not far away."

"OK, Khanh. Tell Bao that we will fire HE (high explosive). Let us know if the rounds are in the right place."

Nago took over and began to drop the small HE rounds in the tube. He yelled instructions for the Nungs to open more rounds and get them ready for him. Jim asked if we could hit the end of the camp with the .50-caliber.

"Good idea, Jim," I said, and we started to take turns firing the big machine gun toward the camp. That must have worked because Khanh came back and said Bao liked the .50.

From our position we had a fairly clear view of the area but couldn't see exactly where the rounds were hitting. The distance was about perfect for the .50. It had a fairly flat trajectory for almost a mile and, with slight elevation, the rounds just cleared the small hooches between us and the edge of town.

Khanh said the VC were moving toward the south, away from the city. I don't know how they had gotten by the ARVNs, unless they were dug in near the PRU camp all along. If they were, they were probably poised to attack Bao when reinforcements arrived. Whatever the situation, it didn't matter now. We spoiled their plans and the VC were definitely on the run.

"Nago, no more 60," I yelled. "We must save ammunition for later."

"We have plenty of .50-caliber rounds, so keep it up," Jim called out over the noisy gun.

Nago stopped firing the mortar and quickly left for more .50-caliber ammunition from our bunker downstairs. If Westy's room wasn't trashed yet, it would be now, I thought, The vibration from the .50 was shaking the entire roof. Westy came up and said the ceiling felt like it was coming down. Jim didn't stop. Whether the gun was effective against the VC or not, he was having a good time and I was sure he thought Westy's room covered with cement was an added bonus.

We kept firing for almost an hour until Bao called and said the VC had gone. A few minutes later we could see a helicopter hunter/killer team working over the area near the border between Chau Doc Province and Long Xuygen Province. They probably were after the same VC we had chased away from the camp. It was approaching dawn and the VC definitely wanted to be some other place when daylight came. If they were caught in the open, they more than likely would be wiped out to the last man.

I was thinking that the ARVNs must be making fairly good progress because there seems to be quite a bit of activity out front. Throughout the night the Nungs were really kept on their toes because the ARVNs would come in from the city and, without identifying themselves, drop off things and or re-supply troops. Whatever the activity was, they were testing the Nungs patience to the maximum.

The friendlies would show up in about any conveyance they had commandeered. Most of the vehicles would stop right in front and, after a bit of commotion, would turn around and head back toward the downtown. I spent most of the night with the Nungs at that position while Jim watched the rear-guard post over the river. Westy liked the roof and walked around with the hand-held air-to-ground radio in his hand, as if it were going to speak to him at any moment. The SEALs positioned themselves strategically throughout the compound and took turns trading off watch duty. Maggie found a good spot and settled in for the night, poking her head out every so often to see what was going on.

When daylight came, Lin came up to us while we were eating and having coffee. He had a disgusted look on his face and said, "Vietnamese soldier die," and pointed to the front of the compound.

We all got up from the table to see what the problem was. In front of the gate, the ARVNs had left five of their dead piled in the passenger compartment of a cyclo, which is the Vietnamese version of a pedi-cab, only much smaller. It was a strange sight, especially since rigor mortis had started to set in and the five forms were competing for position in that tiny compartment.

That didn't bother the Nungs as much as the fact the sun was getting pretty high and it was beginning to get hot. As a result, the bodies were starting to give off a strong, sweet smell that didn't make breakfast go down very easy. I guess the Vietnamese thought we would take care of their dead. Jim told Lin to tell the next Vietnamese they saw to move the dead soldiers to their rear. Jim turned to me saying that he had just gotten a call confirming the estimated time of arrival of the Porter in about an hour to take Sau Be and us to Can Tho.

"Great! I'll get the HT-2 (air-to-ground radio) and take a last-minute look around until the aircraft calls in his approach."

"Sounds good, Drew. I've asked Maggie to go along. She said she'd like to pick up some medical supplies and groceries."

I left and re-supplied myself with a few fresh magazines and a couple of grenades. I knew Can Tho wasn't secure yet and I wasn't sure what we'd find when we arrived. I went to the roof and looked out over the city as I waited for the Porter to call in his approach.

# CHAPTER 12

## DELIVERING
## OUR PRIZE!

The Pilatus Porter is a Swiss-manufactured, single-engine turbo-prop aircraft. It performed exceptionally well, just as though it had been built for Air America.

Nevertheless, it had undergone serious modifications for its present use. Most of them were retrofitted with much larger engines. It, like many other types of aircraft in the Air America inventory, flew routine missions throughout Vietnam and other parts of Southeast Asia. On occasions like this, we could call upon the "company" to support us with operational missions.

I've used them on numerous occasions to insert me and my troops in remote regions or extract us when we needed. The crews were extremely cooperative and never hesitated to go where we wanted. I had gained a tremendous respect for their courage and "can do" attitude. The project I was on didn't give us access to any U.S. military support. The real mission of Air America was to support the civilian components fighting this war. It operated much like any commercial air carrier but was available when called upon to support operations such as the one this day. I had the impression from most of the pilots and crew that they were bored with ordinary flying and when they got a mission to fly for us, they were ready to perform.

I remember the first time I rode with them. It was when I was newly recruited for my current job. Following three days of briefings in Saigon at what was called, the "Old Embassy," I was given a ticket and told to take a company driver and go to the airport. When I got there, I saw a long, rather unruly line of Vietnamese civilians with everything from animals and piles of freight waiting to board scheduled flights.

I got in a line to begin what I thought would be a rather long wait. In a short time a tall, red-headed man dressed in the gray uniform of Air America came up to me.

"Are you Mr. Dix?" he asked.

"Yeah," I responded.

"You don't have to wait in this line," as he stuck out his hand and said, "You're new, aren't you?"

"Does it show?" I asked.

Not replying, he led me out of the noisy terminal.

The two of us climbed into his Pilatus Porter and he called the tower for a mid-field departure. This meant we didn't have to taxi to a runway. It was approved as soon as two F-4's landed. Without further instructions, the pilot put power to the propeller and we left the tarmac from where we were resting. The aircraft rolled less than a hundred feet and lifted off with ease. I was impressed then with the performance of the Porter and continued to be throughout my tour of duty.

I hoped the pilot on this mission to Can Tho with Sau Be was one of the ones I knew. I've never been disappointed yet but this was going to take a bit of tricky maneuvering to get in and out under these conditions. We still didn't know where all of the enemy positions were and what anti-aircraft weapons, if any, they had.

The HT-2 radio interrupted my train of thought as the pilot on the inbound aircraft called without giving his position. "This is Porter (aircraft identification garbled), will be overhead in zero five."

I answered, "Roger, we'll be on the road south of town with smoke."

Both the pilot and I were responding in somewhat guarded phrases in case the enemy was monitoring our frequencies.

"I'll pass overhead and follow you to the pick-up point."

"Roger," I said. "Stay over the river. The VC still have control of some of the city."

He acknowledged as I ran downstairs to let Jim and Maggie know it was in-bound. Nago was already in the Jeep and made room for me so I could drive. Sau Be and two Nungs were already on board. Siew and Lin opened the gate and I pulled out with the second Jeep following close behind with one Nung, Maggie in the right seat and Jim at the wheel.

The road was a straight shot to the pick-up point, only a mile from the house. As soon as we cleared the last hooch and a grove of trees that bordered the road, I stopped the Jeep and popped a yellow smoke grenade. No sooner than I got the smoke out the Porter was on final heading directly for us, without further radio traffic.

The big single-engine aircraft appeared to be hovering as it approached. The pilot, whoever he was, knew what he was doing. As soon as the aircraft touched down, the pilot reversed his engine, causing the aircraft to stop in less than 100 feet. Not needing to get out, the pilot slid the small window back and yelled over the high pitch of the propeller for us to get aboard.

The four of us ran around to the passenger side of the Porter and

I slid the door back, shoving Sau Be through the large opening and motioned toward one of the seats. He had an almost hysterical look on his face. It seemed as if he could panic at any moment. Maggie climbed in after him and took the seat I pointed out for her, just behind Sau Be. Jim got into the right front seat next to the pilot. I sat next to Sau Be where I could keep an eye on him.

It was apparent that Jim knew our pilot from past missions. Over the intercom, Jim introduced the pilot as Whitaker and I waved to him without answering. Jim later told me a little about him. Whitaker was a former crop duster from Tennessee and really knew how to handle light fixed-wing aircraft like the Pilatus Porter or any other type with high power-to-weight ratios.

I was glad we had tied Sau Be's hands. I really didn't want to have to shoot him to keep him from destroying the inside of the aircraft and causing it to crash. I was remembering how hard it was to restrain one other prisoner who literally had gone berserk. It took five of us to control him without doing him serious damage. Sau Be wouldn't have done us any good dead and I sure didn't want to lose him.

I thought it very likely that he had never been in an airplane before. It also occurred to me that maybe he was worried about the short field we were using. We were still on the road and it was too narrow to maneuver the aircraft around to take off toward the direction it had landed. If the pilot could do that, he would have had virtually an unlimited runway. The way he was facing now gave him less than 200 feet before the road turned. Additionally he would have to head toward the city where we could receive enemy fire. I guess the only one who wasn't concerned was the pilot.

Whitaker shouted back before the door was shut, "Hold on, we're rolling." The aircraft started moving before he turned to look forward again. In half the remaining distance, the aircraft was airborne and started a hard-left climbing turn almost immediately. As soon as he cleared some low bushes and other roadside obstacles, he pushed the nose of the aircraft over and hugged the ground to gain more airspeed. We were so close I thought the wheels were going to touch.

The aircraft headed toward the PRU camp and away from the city. Passing over the camp by only a few feet, it was easy to recognize individuals. I saw Bao and I thought I could even detect a very satisfied look on his face as the Pilatus Porter hauled away the prize. Bao was a good soldier but no one argued the fact that he had a strong mercenary streak in him. Sau Be certainly was valuable to our cause, but to Bao he also meant a reward.

It was common practice to reward the PRUs for high-ranking VCs who were captured. We even paid a small bounty for weapons as well. So while the successes we were having over the last several hours were great, they would do much for Bao's personal wealth. While not rich by our standards, Bao was becoming a man of means by Vietnamese standards.

As soon as we gained airspeed, our pilot pointed the aircraft skyward and climbed to a safer altitude. We leveled off at 5,000 feet and settled in for the 45-minute flight.

"Must be a pretty important character," Whitaker said over the intercom.

"Yeah, we think he's pretty high up." Changing the subject, I asked how the situation was in Can Tho.

"It was still pretty screwed up when I left an hour or so ago. The airfield was back in friendly hands but just got that way a few hours before."

"They must be attacking countrywide," I added.

"Yeah, I think so. As soon as I got airborne on my way down here, I picked up a lot of radio chatter from all over. People calling for airstrikes and medivacs. So far there hasn't been much air support. Seems like everyone is up to their asses with their own problems."

"We got that impression when we first called in our situation in Chau Doc."

"Yes, sir, I think Charles (referring to the VC as in Victor Charles for the phonetic alphabet) is on a roll. He hit Can Tho pretty hard and had us in a tailspin for a while. The ARVNs finally got their shit together and took back the city and the airfield. All that is left now are isolated pockets the VC can't get out of.

"The helicopter gunships have really knocked hell out of them and the Vietnamese Air Force were bombing the last positions when I left to come here. When we get closer, keep your eyes open for friendly aircraft. That's our biggest problem right now."

"OK," I responded. "I wish the situation was going that well in Chau Doc. The ARVNs have just started clearing operations. When you guys kick them out of Can Tho, send some more help our way to give us a hand."

"Right! We'll get right on it," Whitaker laughed.

Sau Be, watching the countryside slip by, looked like a man who had just lost his war. The flight seemed to take forever. The Porter was a horse when it came to short-field performance but a real dog when it came to cruise speed. I looked over Whitaker's shoulder and saw the airspeed indicator was struggling to edge past 100.

The flight gave me an opportunity to take a break, and I should have been able to get some sleep; but I couldn't think of sleep with our valuable cargo sitting beside me. I wasn't going to take any chances and I was really pumped up from the last two days.

My thoughts drifted back to the Embassy House, to the SEALs and, especially, Ted. I really hadn't known him that well but I felt sorry for the guys who did. It's tough to lose a close buddy with whom you've gone through so much. I was thinking about the civilians who were so damn lucky and the two Filipinos who almost bought the farm at the CORDs compound.

Then there was Maggie. She looked so intent, sitting there watching the countryside. She had become a good friend of both Jim and me. Maggie was a civilian volunteer nurse who didn't have to be here. She really worked hard, treating mostly Vietnamese civilians at the same hospital we had raced by so many times in the past 50 hours. I wondered if the hospital would ever be put back in good-enough shape for her to work there again.

I shook my head trying to erase all those thoughts from my mind. I needed to think about what we had yet to do and not worry about things I had no control over or that just didn't matter.

In the distance, I began to see smoke on the horizon, which obviously was Can Tho. I tapped on the window and looked back at Maggie and pointed. As we moved closer, our pilot nosed the aircraft over slightly and side-slipped to lose as much altitude as he could in as short of time as possible. We dropped down through the danger area, which was some place between 5,000 feet and the trees. We were now at tree-top level and headed directly for the airfield.

The airfield was adjacent to C-4, the designator for the Special Forces headquarters in the Delta. From what I could see, they were still holed up tight. Their indigenous defenders were at full alert all along the perimeter. The C-Team didn't look at all like the friendly place I'd visited once a month on my way to briefings. I never failed to stop to see some of my Special Forces buddies and have a few beers with them in their club.

Before I was able to prepare myself for the landing, we were on the ground and stopped next to two civilian vehicles that were unmistakably from the Embassy. An American whom I didn't recognize approached us and said, "We can take the prisoner for you."

"No," Jim quickly said. "We'll go with you and turn him over ourselves. We've come too far to let him go now and this place does-n't look all that secure to me."

Jim was right. We've got too much at risk to lose him now. Seeing that Jim meant what he said, the civilian pointed to the second vehicle that was a Ford Bronco. I pushed Sau Be into the front seat and I climbed into the rear next to Maggie so I could keep my eyes on him. He continued to appear calm but a man of his frame of mind could do almost anything, including suicide, in a flash. If that was his choice and he wanted to commit suicide, OK, but I didn't want him to take us along with him.

Jim climbed in with our escort in the lead vehicle. I yelled out of the back to Whitaker, "Wait for us, we won't be very long."

He yelled back that he needed to have clearance for another flight since all aircraft were not flying without Embassy-level approval. Not answering, I waved my acknowledgment out of the back of the Bronco as it sped off.

The ride to the regional office took about 15 minutes. Along the way I could tell that a major battle had been fought here. The streets were deserted except for a few bodies of both VC and GVN soldiers that hadn't been attended to yet. Occasionally we passed a convoy of transport vehicles ferrying soldiers.

There was very little small arms-fire along our route. I could make out in the distance sporadic explosions of rocket fire and the distinct sound of mortars. First I could hear the sound as the rounds were being dropped into the tube and then the report from the explosion a few seconds later. It sounded like the fighting was close due to the short flight of the mortar rounds, much like the situation we had in Chau Doc.

I also could make out what could be the detonation of anti-personnel mines. Then there was the unmistakable sound of mini-guns being fired from Cobra gunships as they circled on the outskirts of town. Probably they were finishing off the escaping enemy forces as they were pushed into the open. They needed to get them now while it's daylight, I thought. If they wait until dark, they won't find a soul. The VC have a way of disappearing in the night.

The two vehicles were waved into the Embassy Compound, which was much larger than ours. We were met outside by Andy Rogers, who was acting as the Regional Officer in Charge (ROIC) while Jim Ward was on leave in the states for the holidays. Andy was a man with a lot of experience of his own. He made quite a reputation for himself behind the lines in the Adriatic countries during WW II with the OSS.

"Hi, Jim and Drew," Andy said, as he greeted us. "You guys have had your hands full it sounds like."

"Yes, sir, we have and you too from what I see," Jim replied.

"Is this your man?" Andy ask, referring to Sau Be.

"Yes, it is," I said. "I can't add anything to the circumstances of his capture that will help you except he was in the middle of the action but unarmed."

Maggie interrupted, not wanting to waste any of the hour and a half Jim allocated her as a condition of coming along. As she turned to leave, Jim said that we would meet her across the street in front of the USAID Headquarters building at noon. We all watched as she half-limped, half-shuffled off, obviously still bothered by her injured knee.

"How did you identify him?" Andy continued.

I replied, "Well, he just looked different so I snatched him up as we went by."

I explained how the VC held their fire momentarily when they saw him. I added, "Do you remember Ba Hung, the high-level guy we have working with the PRUs?"

"Yes, I remember something about him."

"Well Ba Hung recognized him as Sau Be and from what I could tell from my troops, he is something like chief of security for VC An Giang Province."

Jim added, "We thought you should have him. Maybe your interrogation folks could get something out of him."

"Right, Jim. We have some Americans on staff who are fluent in Vietnamese. We'll keep him in our channels as long as we can before we turn him over to the Vietnamese."

"Good!" Jim said. "I hope you can get something out of him. We'd like to get some info back too." He was making the point that we would have liked to had Sau Be for a while but thought he would be more useful at their level and under the control of experienced U.S. interrogators. The fact they were proficient in the language meant that there would be less of a chance that important information would be lost in the translation.

"Maybe he can shed some light on the overall objective of this offensive. Let's hope so, Drew. What do you need from us," Andy asked?

"A little help in Chau Doc would be nice but I'll settle for a ride back to the C-Team. I'd like to see what is going on there intelligence-wise and see if I can scrounge a few things from them."

Not answering, Andy called to one of his men to arrange for me to get back to the airfield and to wait for me while I was at the C-Team. He stuck out his hand and said have a good flight just as if I was going to visit friends in the next town. He called after me as I walked off and said, "Good job up there, Drew."

Jim remained to talk over the situation and called to me that he'd pick up Maggie and meet me at the airfield. I left with my driver without saying a word.

We arrived at the C-Team as two Special Forces sergeants were leading a company-sized indigenous force out the front gate, probably to make a security check of the perimeter. That was a good sign, I thought. The sooner they secure Can Tho, the sooner we can get more help up-river.

As we arrived at the front gate, I was met by a sergeant I knew from Fort Bragg. We exchanged a few words and, seeing that I was in a hurry, he asked what we needed. Not yet knowing what was actually on the Caribou drop, I said that we could always use 9mm and .30-caliber ammunition and grenades. He held up a finger, indicating one minute, and trotted off saying, "I'll see what I can do." In no time he was back with a case of each.

"This will really help us. I'll buy you a beer the next time I'm in town." He helped me toss the three cases in the back of the Bronco. "Matter of fact," I said, "I'll buy you one now. I've got about 20 minutes before I need to leave."

"Can't do that," he said. "I'm on duty here at the gate, but you go ahead. You look like you could use one. A few of the guys you know are in there. They have been on perimeter patrol with the 'indig' all night outside the compound."

"Sounds good but I think I'll go over to S-2 and see if Allard is there. I need to see what intel he's got on the situation in our province." I was referring to Master Sergeant Steve Allard, the C-Team Intelligence sergeant, whom I had gotten to know on the trip from Bragg to Vietnam.

He had proven to be a big help in the past with intel on Chau Doc. He also knew a lot about the political problems between the Vietnamese and Cambodian factions in our province because he had been there on an earlier tour. As inviting as a cool beer sounded, the information I could get from Sergeant Allard would be more useful.

I left the vehicle and driver and headed over to the S-2 shop. After getting the latest information from them, I headed back to the vehicle and proceeded directly to the airfield. Everyone was already there and were loading the supplies and groceries Maggie had requisitioned.

After stowing the ammunition, I hopped in, slid the door shut, claimed my seat next to Maggie and put on my headset. Whitaker, more for conversation, said calmly over the intercom, "Where to?" as he knew we were anxious to get back to Chau Doc. He put the Porter in motion before I was strapped in.

Jim and I were the only ones hooked up with the pilot's intercom. Maggie seemed a little upset as if she had been crying.

I asked Jim what the problem was. He replied, "Maggie just got fired!"

"How can she get fired?" I asked. "She is a volunteer anyway."

He said that when he went to the USAID building to pick her up, she was out front arguing with Lucille, the senior USAID nurse.

"It seems that Lucille didn't want her to go back to Chau Doc until it was secure, he said. "Maggie was trying to tell her that she wanted to go. They were both pretty stubborn. Maggie was determined to come but didn't have a way to get the message across. I guess I helped. I told her if she wanted to come, to come on, the plane is waiting. Maggie left with Lucille hollering after her that she was going to be fired."

Our flight back to Chau Doc was uneventful and this time I was able to get a few minutes sleep. I was relieved that Sau Be was under wraps. After what seemed like just a few minutes, I woke to the pilot saying over the intercom that we'd be in Chau Doc in about 10 minutes: "Do you want to take a look around before we land?"

"Good idea," Jim said.

Whitaker approached high over the PRU camp with the idea that we might stay out of range of small-arms fire just in case the Viet Cong were still in place. After explaining his plan to us, we started a wide left turn around the city. We followed the river for about a mile and the Embassy House came into view.

I called them on the radio and Westy responded, "We're doing pretty good but I'd watch yourselves up there. The VC still hold a few positions down here."

As soon as he answered, we saw a couple of tracers to our left from the direction of the city center. The pilot responded immediately and dropped his right wing and made a descending right turn down to the river. As soon as he completed his turn, we were only a 150 feet over the water. Out of the corner of my eye, I could pick out the PBRs patrolling in the middle of the Bassac.

"I think we've seen enough," I said.

"Me too," Whitaker added and turned the aircraft toward the PRU camp.

""We can land there this time and we'll wait for a ride to the Embassy House."

"Whatever you say, boss."

We touched down in the parking area on the edge of the camp and hopped out. Jim yelled to Whitaker, "Thanks for the lift" and joked about putting it on our tab.

"You know I will," he said laughing and was off again.

Two Jeeps were coming up the road to meet us.

"Jim, I'll stay here a while. I need to talk with Bao."

"We'll go on with the Nungs and take the supplies."

"Take my Jeep too. I'll get a ride with the PRUs.

I spoke to Bao for a few minutes and checked on our wounded. The one with the weird head wound was doing fine; but one of the others had died apparently from shock, which was not all that uncommon.

I went to the man's family and paid my respects. They were with the body and had wrapped it in a straw mat. The man's wife was crying and was extremely emotional. She grabbed my sleeve as if she was pleading for me to do something. She tugged on me to come look at her husband. As she knelt down beside him she uncovered the straw mat from his face and pleaded. Bao, seeing this, interrupted and called for the man's superior to take her away. Bao seemed to always watch over me and didn't want me exposed to her grieving.

The PRUs have had a few casualties since I started with the program. Enough in fact that we had already establish a program, with Jim's concurrence, that any PRU who was wounded, no matter how bad or what physical disability he might incur, could stay at the camp as long as he wanted. We also paid them a small percentage of their monthly salary as a pension. This was great for morale and really didn't amount to much money. The monthly salary for a regular member was just over $30.

Previously, anyone who was badly wounded was on his own after he was injured. Many times the wife had to carry the burden to feed the family.

It worked out well for us. We had improved their morale significantly and since we now had a camp to defend, we had the wounded and their families to help protect it. When the enemy attacked everyone did a job, including the women and children. It was always an all-out defense because not to do so could mean their end.

For those who were KIA, burial expense were paid and their families were given a year's salary in a lump sum. The families also were allowed to stay in the camp as long as they carried their share of the workload. They always stayed because there wasn't much for them on the outside. And the family members, as were the PRU, were definitely considered outsiders by the Vietnamese community because of the nature of their business. If the widow was young, she always managed to find a replacement husband anyway.

It was time for me to go. I had become used to the success I had communicating with Phat and Tran over the past two days and didn't take into account that Bao wasn't tuned into our dialogue. He became frustrated and started looking for someone to translate for us. Not finding anyone right away, he started yelling and ranting and raving, which he often did.

I wasn't sure what he was saying but soon a force of 14 men was standing there ready to go. Whenever Bao went through one of his scenes, he always amazed me. The outcome was just what I wanted but I always felt that Bao had to get the last word in. As I said before, we had developed a very close understanding but he always manipulated his answer to insure that the troops thought it was his idea.

He knew that I knew what his game was. From my point of view it didn't matter. Bao and his men were the best; and as long as we got the job done, whatever it took was OK by me. We quickly started loading up the same Ford pick-up that was shot up earlier. I went around to the front and pointed to the hood. The driver grinned and proudly opened the hood. This time it opened like it was new. The alternator was the same one but somehow they had stitched the housing with wire and taped over it. I had to admit that it looked good.

"Numba one," I said and gave him a slap on the back. "We kill Cong," and I made a firing gesture with my Swedish-K. Neither the driver nor the others left knowing whether we were heading back to do battle with the VC or just take me to the Embassy House. I had to admit I was beginning to like the loyalty that was developing. The driver put the Ford in gear one more time and we sped off toward the Embassy House.

The Embassy House was just as we had left it little more than five hours ago. The same guards were posted on top of the main bunker and they still appeared to be enthusiastic as one scrambled down the ladder to meet me.

"Hello, sir," he said. "Many VC in Can Tho?"

"Yes, there are, but I think the soldiers can take the city back.

Many VC killed."

Siew smiled at that and relayed my report to the others. Nago came running to meet me and said, "Mr. Moore want to see you."

"OK, where is he?"

Nago pointed to the back office and said, "He talk on the radio. Westall there too."

# CHAPTER 13

## LIFE IS GOOD!

There was something missing though. The cyclo with the five bodies was gone.

I asked Vinh, "Soldiers take dead away?"

"No," he said with a sheepish grin and pointed down the road. Off in the distance, a good half-mile away, I saw the cyclo with its grotesque cargo parked under a tree all by itself. The Nungs always knew what needed to be done and took care of things the best way they knew how. I smiled to myself as I walked back to see Jim.

Jim met me halfway on his way from the radio room. He seemed pretty excited as he explained that he had already gotten a preliminary report that Sau Be was going to be very useful. The interrogators already had confirmed that Sau Be was to be the provisional leader of Chau Phu when they kicked us out.

"That's great news, Jim," I replied, also feeling pretty good about it.

"Do you want to take a run through town and see what's going on," Jim asked? "The firing has died down and I talked with the Major Phoung at the TOC and with B-42. They said that it seems like most of the enemy have moved out and the civilians are starting to move around again."

"Sure, Jim, I'll get my Jeep and Nago."

"Good. I'll see if some of the SEALs want to go. They can take Westy's Jeep and follow us. I'm sure they would like to get out for a little sniper patrol. Major Phoung said that the Vietnamese infantry is already assembling to move out of town."

"That was quick work on their part, Jim."

"I guess, Drew, but you guys really cleared out the major strong points for them. All they had to do was move through and hose down the area. I'd like to see how badly the town was hurt during their push."

We loaded up the two Jeeps and of course Harry and Frank were the first to volunteer and climbed onto the rear of my Jeep. Gordy and Jack jumped up into the back of Westy's, along with three more SEALs and we began to leisurely cruise through town. Passing the hospital we saw the tremendous damage inflicted on that structure.

"Maggie isn't going to have much of a place to work, is she, Jim?"

"No, Drew, it sure is screwed up big time."

I retraced my route past the hospital and drove down the street toward the CORDs compound.

"God damn, Drew, that place will never be the same. It took some major hits. Mr. Tull will have to find a different place to work when he gets back from the Philippines."

I continued along the route I had taken several times over the past 56 hours and the realization of what had taken place was starting to sink in. We had really pushed our luck on several occasions, but we didn't have much choice. We came out fairly well considering what we were up against and sure kicked hell out of the VC after they gave us their best shot.

We only lost one U.S. KIA, two PRU KIA, two U.S. wounded and eight PRU wounded. It would be a while before we found out just how bad the VC were hurt. The good thing was that we were able to rescue the eight USAID workers, Major Phoung's wife and children, the two Filipinos and of course we got Maggie out.

Life is good I thought and Jim and I had "our town" back!

The President of the United States of America, authorized by Act of Congress, March 3, 1863, has awarded in the name of The Congress the MEDAL OF HONOR to

STAFF SERGEANT DREW D. DIX
UNITED STATES ARMY

for conspicuous gallantry and intrepidity in action at the risk of his life above and beyond the call of duty:

*Citation:* Staff Sergeant *Drew Dix*, United States Senior Advisor Group, IV Corps, Military Assistance Command, distinguished himself by exceptional heroism while serving as a unit advisor. Two heavily armed Viet Cong battalions attacked the Province capital city of Chau Doc, Republic of Vietnam resulting in the complete breakdown and fragmentation of the defenses of the city. Staff Sergeant *Dix*, with a patrol of Vietnamese soldiers, was recalled to assist in the defense of Chau Phu. Learning that a nurse was trapped in a house near the center of the city, Staff Sergeant *Dix* organized a relief force, successfully rescued the nurse, and returned her to the safety of the Tactical Operations Center. Being informed of other trapped civilians within the city, Staff Sergeant *Dix* voluntarily led another force to rescue eight civilian employees located in a building which was under heavy mortar and small-arms fire. Staff Sergeant *Dix* then returned to the center of the city. Upon approaching a building, he was subjected to intense automatic rifle and machinegun fire from an unknown number of Viet Cong. He personally assaulted the building, killing six Viet Cong, and rescuing two Filipinos. The following day Staff Sergeant *Dix,* still on his own volition, assembled a 20-man force and though under intense enemy fire cleared the Viet Cong out of the hotel, theater, and other adjacent buildings within the city. During this portion of the attack, Army Republic Vietnam soldiers inspired by the heroism and success of Staff Sergeant *Dix*, rallied and commenced firing upon the Viet Cong. Staff Sergeant *Dix* captured 20 prisoners, including a high ranking Viet Cong Official. He then attacked enemy troops who had entered the residence of the Deputy Province Chief and was successful in rescuing the official's wife and children. Staff Sergeant *Dix's* personal heroic actions resulted in 14 confirmed Viet Cong killed in action and possibly 25 more, and the capture of 20 prisoners, 15 weapons, and the rescue of the 14 United States and free world citizens. The heroism of Staff Sergeant *Dix* was in the highest tradition and reflects great credit upon the United States Army.

**THE WHITE HOUSE**
January 16, 1969

# EPILOGUE

It must be said that life around River City, as Chau Phu was called, continued at a fast pace for many months following the fifty-six hours of the Jan 31-Feb 1, 1968, Tet offensive.

I had the good fortune to operate on numerous occasions with the same SEAL platoon and two other SEAL platoons that came to Chau Doc looking for some action. In fact the word got out that our province was not so pacified after all. Some of the operations we conducted together were just as exciting and as successful and certainly no less important than those fifty-six hours of Tet.

I selected the Tet offensive as my subject because it provided me with an excellent vehicle to explain the program I was working with during the most critical period of the war. I strongly believe that in order to be effective in guerrilla wars such as that, you have to have units made up of indigenous troops like the PRU to get the job done.

Unfortunately the United States tried to fight a political war with conventional soldiers. Don't get me wrong. We had the finest troops in the world and seldom lost a battle, but it takes more than winning battles and body count to win a war. You've got to get to the enemy's core and pluck it out!

I attempted to identify the problem we had with leadership in the ARVN ranks by explaining the breakdown in the leadership during Tet. This doesn't mean that all Vietnamese leaders were ineffective. On the contrary, many were great. The great ones just didn't last long. After all we were expecting them to fight until they were killed.

The Americans were usually sent back to the States in a year, leaving the local leaders to continue, often with a fresh new counterpart ready to win the war! That war just went on too long. We gave the enemy all the time it needed to build and train its army. When they needed more time, we simply found a way to give it to them.

The "Professionals" in the unconventional and special operations units were starting to run out as well. The reader should take the time to investigate the numbers of special operations personnel who were either killed in action or missing in action while serving with indigenous troops. The numbers will appall you.

Keep in mind that often only one or two U.S. Special Forces personnel were leading large numbers of indigenous troops, which kept the number of U.S. casualties down. As I've said before, while we'll always have "Professionals" willing and very eager to do the job, their numbers eventually will run out after a number of years. I can't remember all of the names of the men I knew who were killed. Certainly almost everyone I know has been wounded!

The people in "The Rescue of River City" were special. Each had a desire to be part of something great before they even went to Vietnam. I'm sure that they kept up the momentum after they left that country.

When the communists overran South Vietnam in 1975 they immediately replaced the South Vietnamese government officials with their own. This transition went fairly rapidly in most of the country with the exception of the Delta. There they had more of a problem for the same reasons we had in securing the area from them.

The people were just as difficult for the communists to deal with. Bao and others like him moved into the very familiar strongholds that the Viet Cong used to operate from. Bao and several of his men holed up in Nui Coto, one of the Seven Mountains in Chau Doc Province, and conducted a long but futile fight against the new government. I was able to sponsor several of the Chinese Nungs, including Nago and Ba Hung, the former VC who identified Sau Be, when they left Vietnam. Through them I was able to keep in touch with what was happening back in Chau Doc long after the takeover.

I often met with my former troops in Fayetteville, N. C. At one of those meetings, a few years after the takeover, Ba Hung, with his limited knowledge of English, made an attempt to explain Bao's situation. He had tears in his eyes when he told me that the communists had killed Bao. This was unusual since Ba Hung was very stoic and seldom said much.

He explained how Bao's sister had notified him that the communists were willing to grant amnesty to him and his men if he came in from hiding and turned himself in. Bao either believed her or he was just weary of the many years of combat. I've never really understood why, but he came to Chau Doc and surrendered. The officials immediately took him to the market square where he was promptly executed.

I knew how Ba Hung felt. It was a humiliating way for a warrior to go and I often think of him!

# ACKNOWLEDGEMENT

I've come to realize that I've been extremely fortunate to have had the opportunity to work with some of the finest people in the world. It's not the units we serve in that were so great but the people in those units with us.

It's all of those people who I must acknowledge for making this book possible. I regret that it is not possible to thank each of them for their influence on me. For some it was the simply fact of an instructor not letting up during rigorous training when it would have been so easy to do so. I thank them for being the animals we thought they were at the time.

I thank my training buddies who gave each other encouragement when it would have been easy to call it quits; and I especially thank those soldiers who never quit on the battlefield and held their end of the line when it would have been easy to not do so. But then again, I don't know many who would have done less. Without them. many of us wouldn't be here to write about such things.

I am grateful for the many hours on the phone with good friends and authors before me. Bob Gormly, a combat buddy who wrote "Combat Swimmer," and Dick Couch, who wrote "Seal Team One", convincing me that I had a story to tell.

Colonel David Hackworth was especially helpful walking me through the publishing arena.

My good friend Ruben Archuleta, former Chief of Police in Pueblo, Colo., and author of " I came from El Valle" was a big help in getting me started on the self-publishing route. He loaded me up with lots of written information on the subject.

Pete Lemon, a Medal of Honor recipient and author of "Beyond the Medal" was most enthusiastic and encouraging about my project.

Most of all, many thanks to my brother, Jay Dix, an author and publisher who has been great in directing me to the right places to get things done.

Everyone needs good, honest friends to rely on for the first reading of the draft manuscript. If it had not been for them, I wouldn't have been able to get the feeling that my message was getting across. It's simply too tough to read your own work.

Many thanks to my first reader and sounding board, Patricia, my wife. We spent many long and sometimes uncomfortable moments as she checked me out on the laptop. Both of us owe a great deal to Phil Ruegg, the computer expert at the Pueblo Chieftain for making our software do what we needed.

Thanks to my good friend Joe Faulhaber from Fairbanks, Alaska., for taking the time to read and give me still another perspective.

The input of "Gunfighter" Lieutenant General Hank Emerson was important. His opinion meant a lot to me as he is a soldier's hero!

A special thanks goes to Barclay Jameson, my copy editor who was also one of the first to read the story. Since this was my first attempt at writing, his input had a special meaning. I met him when he was the executive editor for my hometown newspaper, "The Pueblo Chieftain". I'm thankful he just retired from the paper so he had the time to help me with my grammar and punctuation.

A special thanks also goes to my combat buddies I didn't write about, wherever they are and to those still in Vietnam!

# GLOSSARY

**A-TEAM-** The primary field element of the Special Forces. An A-Team is comprised of twelve men and has the primary mission to organize, train and lead indigenous troops against their enemies.

**AK-47-** A Russian or Chinese manufactured, fully automatic, assault rifle, used throughout the world by communist supported armies. It was the primary weapon of the Viet Cong main force infantry units during the Vietnam War. It had a thirty round magazine and fired a 7.62 Russian bullet.

**ARVN-** Was the acronym for the Army of Vietnam. Vietnamese units were often referred to as ARVN's.

**B-40-** Was the term used for the projectile that was fired from a Communist Rocket propelled grenade launcher. It was designed primarily as an anti-tank weapon but was also used as an anti-personnel weapons and for knocking out fortified positions.

**B-42-** The numerical designation for the Special Forces B Team in Chau Doc Province. B Teams were the command and support element over A Teams, which were the primary combat element of the Special Forces. There were several B teams in Vietnam. The "4" designation in 42 ,meant that it was in the Fourth Corps.

**BATTALION-** An American infantry unit of approximately six to eight hundred men. There usually are four company-sized units in a US battalion and support elements needed to support the ground maneuver force. Viet Cong Battalions were usually much smaller, approximately three hundred including support units.

**BLACK PJAMMAS-** Clothing often worn by the indigenous farmers in Vietnam. Because of their popularity, the Viet Cong often wore them as well either as a military uniform or to confuse their enemy as to their true role.

**BOSTON WHALER-** A fiberglass boat manufactured in the United States primarily for civilian use. It usually had an open cockpit and is noted for being very stable and suitable for large outboard motors.

**BMNT-** Beginning morning nautical twilight is the time of day, just before sunrise where a person can see approximately 400 meters.

**C-TEAM-** The designation for the primary command and support element for Special Forces units. The B- Teams and A- Teams were under the C-Team respectively.

**CAMMIES-** The short term used for camouflaged uniforms.

**CARIBOU-** A twin engine Canadian manufactured aircraft, also known as a C7-A, manufactured by De Havilland. Ideally suited for rough terrain and air drops.

**CLAYMORE BAG-** A handy canvas bag that a claymore anti-personnel mine came in. Often used to carry miscellaneous equipment by the combat soldier.

**CLICK-** A common term used by ground troops to mean kilometer

**E&E-** Evasion and escape is the term used for training military personnel in the art of evasion from the enemy and escape if captured. The term is often used by special operations personnel to identify a route to be used if over run or isolated during behind the lines missions.

**COMPANY-** An army US ground unit of approximately one hundred and fifty men. About four companies comprised an infantry battalion. Viet Cong companies were much smaller.

**GVN-** Acronym for the Government of Vietnam. Often used generically to identify different entities of fighting units i.e. A GVN army platoon.

**EMBASSY HOUSE-** Was the term used to describe the headquarters and/or base of operations in each Provincial Capital for the paramilitary operations programs conducted by the Central Intelligence Agency in Vietnam.

**FLARES-** Illumination round fired to provide ground elements increased visibility during the night. They come in all configurations and are fired either by hand or from mortars or artillery. Some are dropped from aircraft. Most have a parachute attached that allows the burning flare to descend slowly.

**HE-** The acronym for high explosive. HE mortar rounds are those that detonate and explode on the target with the primary purpose to destroy the target by the force of the explosion and/ or the shrapnel from the disintegrating projectile.

**HOOCHES**- Was the term used by the US military personnel to describe the small houses used by the indigenous people all over Vietnam and other parts of the region.

**IV CORPS**- One of the four regional Military divisions of South Vietnam. I CORPS was the northern most while IV CORPS was the southern most.

**INDIGENOUS**- Means the local population with in Vietnam or any country. The term "indig" is simply the shortened version of the term.

**KIA**- Killed in action.

**LAMBROS**- Noisy and smoky, three wheeled motorized vehicles built on the order of a motor scooter with a cargo bed that could carry about ten Vietnamese or freight.

**LZ**- Is the abbreviation for landing zone. A cleared area suitable for landing helicopters.

**M-26**- The military designation for the US hand grenade. It is designed to kill or wound the enemy by fragmentation, i.e., fragmentation grenade.

**M-60**- Is the standard machine-gun used today by US forces and during the Vietnam War. It fires a 7.62 millimeter round.

**M-79 GRENADE LAUNCHER**- was a US weapon used during the time that fired a single 40MM round that exploded on impact much like a hand grenade.

**MISSION ORDERS-** The term used to describe orders given to subordinates with the greatest flexibility to get the job done.

**MORTAR-** An indirect fire weapon carried and used by the infantry for it's own artillery support. Indirect fire means that the weapon is fired at a high angle when the round is dropped into a tube. When the round strikes the bottom of the tube the projectile is propelled out toward the target, exploding on impact with the ground or if firing illumination round explodes in the air dispensing a parachute flare.

**MONKEY BRIDGE**- A very crude bridge constructed by the locals to cross small canals or ponds. Usually a one- pole footbridge supported by flimsy support post driven in the ground. Some were only ten- twelve feet long while others could span several meters. A vulnerable spot for an ambush.

**PBR-** A thirty-two foot fiberglass navy boat, with a crew of five, used primarily for river interdiction operations and for inserting combat troops. They were heavily armed with twin fifty- caliber machine - guns on the bow. On the stern any number of weapons could be mounted depending on the mission such as a light machine-gun or hand cranked .40 mm grenade launcher, called a Honeywell. Some carried a mortar.

**PIASTER-** Vietnamese currency.

**PLATOON-** An infantry unit of approximately thirty or forty men. There usually are three or four, ten man, squad-sized elements in a platoon.

**POINTMAN-** Was the designation for the front man in a column of troops moving in a combat formation. The point man was usually a fairly seasoned person that was trail wise. If enemy contact were made, the pointman would usually be the first to initiate contact and almost always the first to receive fire. He had the mission to avoid mines and to alert the rest of the patrol of enemy activity and/or obstacles.

**POW-** Prisoner of war.

**PRC-25-** A portable FM radio used by ground personnel to communicate between elements.

**S-2-** The military staff responsible for intelligence.

**SAMPAN-** A small, wooden, shallow draft, water- craft, operated by local civilians. They were usually round bottomed, ideally suited for use in the inland waterways. The smallest were about eight to ten feet and carried three people. The largest could be more than thirty-five feet and carried several people. The smaller ones were usually non-powered and were poled along by an operator standing in the rear. Some were engine driven and moved very efficiently over the water.

**SEAWOLVES-** Was the name given to the US Navy helicopter gun-ships. They were converted troop helicopters armed with rockets and 7.62mm machine guns. The SEALs almost always had them at their disposal when deployed in the field. They had the reputation of being there when they were needed and have been credited for saving many lives.

**SEAL-** The acronym for the Navy's sea, air, land elite troops, with the mission to provide the Navy with reconnaissance and ground special mission capabilities near the water.

**SPECIAL OPERATIONS-** The mission beyond the capabilities of conventional military forces. Special operations missions include sabotage, reconnaissance beyond the area influenced by conventional forces, capture and recovery and anything that the major commanders need to be done.

**STARLIGHT SCOPE-** A US made device that had tremendous light gathering characteristics. It was developed during the Vietnam war and during the early years of the war was considered classified and as a result, the first units that had them were special operations troops.

**STONER-** Was a weapon used by the SEALs during the Vietnam war. It was a shoulder type weapon that fired the same 5.56 cal round used in the M-16 but was belt fed and operated similar to a machine-gun only much lighter.

**SWEDISH-K** - Also know as the Carl Gustav sub-machine gun. Manufactured in Sweden, it was of World War II vintage and fired the 9MM round. Many non-military programs purchased them on the civilian market as they were readily available.

**TACTICAL OPERATIONS CENTER (TOC)-** Is the term used by the military for the major command element of a conventional military operation. It is the place where major field staff was located and also where most of the communications used to control the battlefield elements was located.

**THERMITE GRENADE-** An incendiary grenade type device that produces an extremely hot fire used to melt through metal such as in an artillery breech, an engine block or a safe. It is seldom thrown but placed on the piece to be destroyed.

**UNCONVENTIONAL WARFARE-** The mission to organize, train and lead indigenous forces in battle against their or our enemy. Unconventional warfare includes tactics used by conventional forces as well as conducting special operations missions with indigenous forces any place in the world.

**WIA-** Wounded in action.

For ordering information
contact Drew Dix publishing web site at:
**www.drewdix.com**